# From Passive to Assertive

## 5 Simple Steps

By
**Corinne Coe**

QLD, Australia
MMXXIV

Copyright © Corinne Coe 2024
QLD, Australia
MMXXIV
www.corinnecoe.com

Corinne Coe has asserted her right under the Copyright, Designs and Patents Act 1988 to be identified to be the author of this book.

This book is a work of non-fiction based on life, experience and recollections of the author and in some cases those who have gone before. In some cases, names of people have been changed to protect the privacy of others. The author states that, except in such respects the content of this book is accurate and true according to her memory of events.

The author of this book does not dispense medical advice or prescribe the use of any technique as a form of treatment for physical, emotional, or medical problems without the advice of a physician either directly or indirectly. The 'intent' of the author is only to offer information of a general educative nature to help you in your quest for emotional and psychological well-being. In the event you use any of the information in this book for yourself, which is your constitutional right, the author and publisher assume no responsibility for your actions.

All rights reserved. No part of this publication may be reproduced, stored in a retrieval system, or transmitted in any form or by any means electronic, medical, photocopying, recording, or otherwise, without the prior written permission of the author.

First published in Australia in its current form in 2024
by Corinne Coe.
ISBN 978-0-9946461-1-8

Cover design by Angelica Mioche
Typesetting by *LimeSpringStudio.com*

For my parents, thank you for teaching me important life skills, including assertiveness skills.

"Walls keep everybody out. Boundaries teach them where the door is."

—MARK GROVES

# CONTENTS

What Does It Mean To Be Assertive? ........................ 6

Why Do We Find It Difficult To Be Assertive With Others? .................................................................... 22

What Is Aggressive And Passive Behaviour? .......... 39

How To Become Assertive ....................................... 71

Applying The Assertive Formula ............................. 89

Being Assertive In Your Relationships ................... 109

Being Assertive In The Workplace ......................... 141

How To Assert Yourself With Difficult People ... 166

Conclusion .............................................................. 195

# 1.

## *What does it mean to be assertive?*

The importance of having assertiveness skills for our mental and physical well-being, healthy relationships, and overall happiness and peace is often undervalued. Without assertiveness skills, life can be more challenging than necessary. In most situations, the people in your life make it difficult and unpleasant, not life itself. Is it your job that is the problem, or is it your boss, your co-workers, or the customers? Is the social situation difficult, or is it that difficult person? Is the course the problem, or is it the lecturer? If you take the time to reflect on your past and pinpoint all of the situations that you found challenging, and then ask yourself, "Was it the person involved in that situation or the situation itself that was the challenging part?" you'd most probably conclude that the person/s in every situation was the problem, not the situation, activity, or task. As you can see, the people in your life are making your life more problematic and negative than it needs to be. Don't get me wrong, assertive people have to deal with difficult people in their lives, too; the difference is that they just don't 'allow' them to affect them or their lives. When you are assertive, you are armed against toxic and difficult people. You will only attract people who are also assertive and will respect you, your needs, and your feelings, just like they would expect from you. Assertive people attract other assertive people with whom they can have a genuine and respectful relationship. Now that you understand the important role of assertiveness in your life and overall well-being, it's important to grasp the true meaning of being 'assertive'. Assertiveness is often mistaken for aggressiveness, discouraging people from learning this crucial life skill. As you will soon discover, assertiveness is actually the opposite of aggressiveness.

Assertiveness is a skill that can be learned. It involves standing up for your rights and expressing your thoughts, feelings, and beliefs directly, honestly, respectfully, and appropriately without violating the other person's rights and beliefs. In other words, both parties should feel positive and respected at the end of an assertive conversation. This mutual respect is a key aspect of assertiveness, ensuring that both parties feel understood and valued.

**No one should be left feeling:**
- Threatened
- Confused
- Attacked
- Guilty
- Blamed
- Hurt
- Defensive
- Angry
- Manipulated
- Anxious or
- Made to feel any negative emotion at the end of an assertive conversation.

**Assertiveness is:**
- Recognising and expressing needs, feelings, and opinions, negative and positive.
- Asking clearly and directly for what you want.
- Saying 'no' politely and establishing boundaries.

- Let go of old behaviour patterns, unrewarding relationships, and situations.
- Taking responsibility for your feelings and actions, and using 'I' statements.
- Respecting yourself: listening to what your body is telling you.
- Respecting other people and listening to them.
- Being prepared to compromise to resolve conflict.
- Setting goals and planning steps to achieve them.
- Empowering others and wanting them to be happy.

**Assertiveness** involves standing up for your personal rights and expressing your thoughts, feelings, and beliefs in a direct, honest, and appropriate way that does not violate another person's rights. It also means respecting not only your own needs and rights but also the needs and rights of others.

**Assertiveness** is an alternative to passive, aggressive, and manipulative behaviour. It is not to be confused with aggressive behaviour as it sometimes is.

Now that you understand what it means to be assertive, you can assess your level of assertiveness by taking the Assertiveness Test at the end of this chapter. To identify areas for improvement, you need to recognise the changes you need to make and the areas of strength you can build on. Taking the test will help you see the situations, people, and areas where you are not being assertive.

## "Why is assertiveness so important?"

When assertive, you are more likely to be treated respectfully, fairly, and appropriately by people. Therefore, you are more likely to feel valued and worthy. Feeling valued and respected by others is important for developing healthy self-esteem and self-worth. Self-esteem is the overall evaluation or appraisal of one's worth. It is our opinion of ourselves, including the beliefs and emotions we have about ourselves. High self-esteem leads to confidence and competence in dealing with life's challenges and feeling secure. On the other hand, low self-esteem leads to feeling useless, unprepared for life, and not feeling equal to others. There is also sufficient evidence to suggest that self-esteem is crucial for maintaining mental and physical well-being and healthy relationships.

## Assertiveness Will Improve Your Self-Esteem

The relationship between self-esteem and assertiveness is quite significant. You need a strong sense of self-worth to be comfortable enough to be assertive, which also helps maintain a high sense of self-worth. From a young age, we are taught the importance of being liked and accepted by everyone, which can sometimes make us feel inadequate when faced with disapproval. By the end of this book, you will realise the irrationality of expecting always to be liked, no matter how hard you try. Relying on others' opinions and treatment to determine our self-worth can damage our self-esteem. Assertiveness is crucial in maintaining and developing self-esteem by ensuring we are treated as we deserve. Without assertiveness, you are at a greater risk of attracting people into your life who will not only harm your self-esteem but also have a negative impact on your health, well-being, and happiness. Assertiveness is essential for attracting the right people into your life – those who will support you in developing and maintaining strong self-esteem and living a healthy, well-adjusted life.

## Assertiveness Will Improve Your Relationships

Assertive individuals tend to attract other assertive and confident individuals into their lives. When you are assertive, you will only attract people who appreciate your assertiveness and are confident and assertive. These individuals will value your honesty, openness, and direct and upfront communication style. Why? Because they want to achieve the same positive outcome as you without the typical complications that can often arise when trying to communicate with a non-assertive person. When you are assertive with another assertive person, no complications or misunderstandings can stand in the way of your relationship with them. Effective communication is effortless and free of stress. Both parties can easily achieve their communication goals when they are assertive and active listeners. Good communication fosters healthy relationships, whether they are personal or work-related. When both parties can openly express their feelings and needs without fear of judgment, resolving any issues between them becomes much easier.

## Being assertive will prevent you from over-committing and constantly trying to please others.

Stress occurs when the demands placed on us exceed our ability to cope, leading to physical and psychological strain. Overcommitting and people-pleasing can add to stress, and while it's something many of us are aware of, it can be difficult to change these habits. Have you ever promised yourself that you would say "no" next time, only to find yourself saying "yes" again? Have you ever been told by others that it's easy to say "no," but found it difficult to do so yourself? This may be because others are more assertive and not afraid of saying "no" because they are not worried about being disliked or rejected. They understand that they have the right to refuse. Assertive individuals understand their rights and recognise that those who refuse to treat them fairly and respectfully are not meant to be a part of their lives. They believe that they are entitled to the same rights that they afford to others. Therefore, it's important to note that constantly trying to please others and overcommitting does not attract genuine people into your life. Instead, it only draws those who seek to take advantage of you. How many times have you continuously given to people, in one form or another, only to end up getting deeply hurt by them? How much more time are you willing to spend grieving over the loss of not only your friendships and relationships and the time you have invested in the wrong people? As I mentioned earlier, it's not easy to say "no" when you're not assertive. However, by the end of this book, you will be more assertive, and your life will change for the better.

## Being assertive helps you effectively communicate and meet your needs.

Being assertive means clearly asking for what you want in a way that leaves no room for misunderstanding. Assertive people understand their rights and know it's reasonable and fair to ask for what they need. They also recognise that their needs are as important as anyone else's and deserve the same consideration and respect. Meeting your needs means asking the people in your life to accept you unconditionally, allow you to be your true self, and consider your feelings, values, and needs. Assertive individuals are unafraid to express themselves because they surround themselves with like-minded people who are confident and appreciate their differences. If you fail to communicate your needs for happiness and health, you will always feel undervalued, unappreciated, and unconditionally unaccepted. Life is not solely about prioritising others' happiness at your own expense. If your values, interests, and needs are not fulfilled, you merely conform to others' expectations and are not true to yourself. Assertiveness can guide you to discover your true self and find your voice.

Your connections with others are incredibly important for your self-worth and overall well-being. We often judge ourselves based on how others see us, regardless of their true opinions. This is why selecting individuals in your life who will value and embrace the confident new you and will reciprocate the same respect and consideration that you extend to them is crucial. Assertiveness is an important skill to have for your well-being, health, and happiness. It creates opportunities for personal growth and allows you to live a comfortable life as your true self. By being assertive, you gain a better understanding of yourself and others, leading to healthier relationships. It empowers you to shape a life that aligns with who you are, rather than trying to fit into a life that doesn't suit you. Assertiveness also serves as a shield against mistreatment, helping to boost your self-esteem and self-confidence. Assertiveness acts like a 'filter' in our life. Let me explain how.

When assertive, we avoid drama and harm by keeping "toxic" people out. It's our responsibility to screen the people who try to come into our lives to protect our self-esteem and well-being. If someone does not respond positively to your assertiveness, that person is not someone you want in your life because they will likely cause you a lot of grief. Remember: when you are being assertive, you are simply asking for respect in a tactful manner. This should lead to a positive response from others. If they do not respond positively, you have likely avoided involvement with a toxic person. The power of assertiveness in our lives is often underestimated. It's often better to keep a person in your life whom you have no choice but to have at arm's length rather than getting too involved with them and being constantly dragged into their drama. Consider redefining your relationship with them to just an 'acquaintance' level if necessary. "Toxic" doesn't just refer to people who intentionally try to harm you but also to those who have personal issues they can't control, which can negatively affect you if you let them. So, using assertiveness skills in every aspect of your life protects your self-esteem and helps evaluate the quality of your relationships.

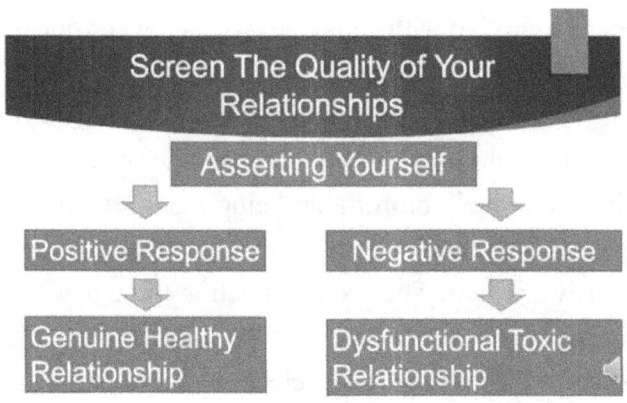

## Why can we be assertive in some situations but not in others?

It is common for people to find it easier to be assertive with certain individuals in their lives and not with others. You may find that you can be assertive with your partner and/or your children but not with your friends or work colleagues, or vice versa. Although this may indicate that you are an assertive person who is not applying assertion to other areas of your life, it's not always the case. It's important to note that anyone can appear assertive when dealing with someone who is too passive or lacks the confidence to assert themselves. You might think you are assertive, but if you can't apply your assertiveness skills with other people in your life and different situations, you may not actually be assertive. Anyone can be assertive with someone who is not confident or assertive enough to stand up for themselves. If you find it difficult to be assertive in all aspects of your life, it might simply be because the people with whom you feel comfortable being assertive are 'safe' for you. This doesn't necessarily mean that you are an assertive person. There's a distinction to be made. An assertive person can be assertive with anyone in any situation. They are not selective about who they choose to be assertive with because they have the skills and the confidence to use these skills in any situation and with anyone. You may feel confident and have the basic assertiveness skills to deal with less challenging situations and people, but you may lack the confidence or assertiveness skills to handle more challenging situations and people. There are various reasons why individuals struggle to assert themselves. These reasons will be detailed in the following chapter.

> ✏️ **Complete Activity 1.0**
> **How Assertive Am I? – Test**

Although this is not a validated psychological scale or test, it can help you determine your assertiveness. Place a ✓ tick next to the statements you feel very comfortable with and a ✗ cross next to the statements that make you uncomfortable.

- ☐ Speaking out and asking questions at a meeting

- ☐ Stating your views to an authority figure (boss, therapist, parent)

- ☐ Making clear decisions vs. doing what others think you should do.

- ☐ Requesting expected service when you haven't received it.

- ☐ Choosing to do what is right for you without guilt, despite another's manipulation.

- ☐ Respecting your own needs as much as or more than others do theirs.

- [ ] Being expected to apologise for something but not apologising since you feel you are in the right.

- [ ] Setting your standards based on your unique style and personality.

- [ ] Respecting your limits and preventing the Superwoman or Superman Syndrome

- [ ] Talk about your talents and triumphs openly and comfortably without embarrassment.

- [ ] Looking in the mirror with a genuine smile and saying to yourself, "I like you".

- [ ] Accepting a rejection.

- [ ] Receiving a compliment by saying something assertive to acknowledge that you agree with the person.

- [ ] Telling someone that they are doing something that is bothering you.

- [ ] Discussing a person's criticism openly with them.

- [ ] Saying 'no' to a favour you don't want to do.

- [ ] Telling a person when he or she is manipulating you.

- ☐ Expressing anger directly and honestly when you feel angry.

- ☐ Disciplining your children.

- ☐ Initiating a discussion with your boss about a raise or promotion.

- ☐ Refusing to do your boss' personal errands or shopping.

- ☐ Accepting performance feedback from your boss, even when it is negative.

- ☐ Being able to say no when asked to take on one more extra project "for the sake of your career".

- ☐ Accepting a challenge and sticking with it.

- ☐ Taking a courageous stand even if it is personally or politically.

**If you have more crosses than ticks, you would definitely benefit from developing your assertiveness skills.**

# 2.

## *Why do we find it difficult to be assertive with others?*

There are various reasons why we may struggle to be assertive with others. The most common reasons include: We do not believe we have the right to be assertive.

- We do not believe we are worthy of the same rights we give others.

- We do not know how to be assertive.

- We were conditioned in childhood to be submissive.

- Fear of losing control.

Let's review each of these reasons in greater detail.

## We do not believe that we have the right to be assertive

To be assertive, knowing and accepting your rights in your personal and work life is important. Being assertive allows you to act in your best interests, stand up for yourself without undue anxiety, and express your honest feelings comfortably. It also enables you to express your personal rights without denying the rights of others. To accomplish this, you must first understand what your personal and work rights are, and you must acknowledge that you deserve to have these same rights. Many people find it easy to accept these rights for others, but their actions show that they do not accept them for themselves. For instance, we may be overly tolerant and quick to make excuses for others.

> *"She probably didn't realise what she was doing…"*

But we don't always make these same allowances for ourselves!

> *"I'm 40 years old. You'd think I would have learned by now…"*

Why don't we give ourselves the same rights we give others? There are several reasons for this, but the most common are low self-esteem, perfectionism, and conditioning. You might be aware of your personal and work rights, but you might not feel worthy enough to apply these rights to yourself. Perfectionism can also be a barrier to exercising your rights. When you have high standards and expect nothing less than 100%, you will probably find applying these rights to your personal and work life very difficult. For example, you are more likely to be harder on yourself than others when you make a mistake. Another barrier is conditioning, often developed in childhood due to a highly critical and punitive upbringing. If we are repeatedly told throughout our lives that we do not deserve the same rights as others, we will eventually believe it and carry this belief into adulthood. These barriers will be explained in more detail later on.

## We do not believe that we deserve the same rights as others.

As mentioned earlier, poor self-esteem is one of the

most common barriers to assertiveness. You learned earlier how healthy self-esteem and assertiveness go hand in hand. What you may not know is the important role of assertiveness in asserting your personal rights. How can you exercise your rights when you do not believe you deserve them? Regardless of the experiences you may have had in your life, the mistakes you have made, or how others have treated you throughout your life – you are a worthy person. Most negative experiences do not happen because we deserve them but because we have allowed them to happen to us. If you were to judge yourself only on who you are as a person and not solely on what you have been told by the minority of people that you have had dealings with throughout your life, you would find out that you are not as bad as you believe you are. You possess many of the same qualities as others, such as honesty, trustworthiness, love, care, consideration, and kindness, making you a good person overall. Therefore, there should be no difference between you and anyone else in terms of deserving equal rights. Everyone deserves the same rights of respect and consideration. You should believe that you are just as deserving of these rights as you believe others are.

## We lack the skills of assertiveness.

As mentioned in the previous section, some individuals possess the skills to be assertive but lack the confidence to apply them. These individuals may know what they want to say and may even be aware of their personal and work rights, but they may lack the confidence to express themselves. On the other hand, for most non-assertive individuals, the issue lies in not having the skills of assertiveness. They are unaware of the correct way or the appropriate words to convey their message assertively. The ability to assert oneself requires specific techniques. Without knowledge of these techniques, being assertive can be challenging. However, once these techniques are learned, assertiveness becomes much easier. This book will teach you these essential skills.

## We were Conditioned in Childhood to be Submissive

If our parents and teachers taught us to be submissive and prioritise other people's needs and feelings over our own, we may struggle with being assertive as adults. Assertiveness is a skill that we should learn during childhood, teenage, and young adult years, so if assertive parents raised us, we are more likely to be assertive individuals. If you had dominant and/or submissive parents or other significant mentors in your life, you might not have had the opportunity to develop assertiveness skills. We tend to observe and learn from those who influence us most. As a result, we may develop certain behaviours, such as non-assertive or even aggressive communication styles, to cope and survive. People who have experienced violence and abuse are more likely to develop a fear of conflict, which can make it difficult for them to be assertive later in life. When you have been traumatised, you may carry that fear and lack of trust into your adult life. If avoiding conflict helped you escape harm in the past, you are also likely to avoid conflict in your adult life. Fear of conflict is a common factor that prevents people from being assertive, and we will discuss this later.

## Fear of Losing Control

Another conditioned behaviour is the fear of standing up for ourselves and being backed into a corner, which can make us feel foolish. Some people are passive-aggressive. They start off by letting things go because they fear not getting the response they want from the other person. However, they may eventually lash out because they can no longer tolerate the other person's behaviour. This behaviour can harm relationships, so passive-aggressive individuals are very selective about who they are aggressive towards. They often tolerate the behaviour of assertive or aggressive people because they don't want to appear foolish or weak, and they can be aggressive towards passive individuals because they feel assured of winning. Their goal is to avoid being seen as weak or passive. This behaviour typically develops early in life and is influenced by early experiences. The need to be accepted is also a conditioned response. Suppose we did not feel unconditionally accepted in our early life. In that case, we are more likely to seek acceptance from others in adulthood and less likely to want to take the risk of asserting ourselves for fear of being rejected. This is a common barrier to being assertive. People who constantly seek acceptance and reassurance from others are prepared to sacrifice their rights and feelings to avoid the feeling of rejection that they may have experienced in childhood.

Ensuring that our expectations of others are reasonable involves granting them the same rights we expect for ourselves. Similarly, we should ensure that our expectations of ourselves are realistic and that we afford ourselves the same rights we are willing to give to others. So, what personal and work rights do we need to incorporate into our lives? Let's begin with the rights we should apply to our personal lives and relationships.

## Your Personal Rights

The rights mentioned may seem ordinary and acceptable at first, but it can take a long time for some of these rights to truly resonate with you and for you to accept them for yourself and others.

## My rights as a person

1. I have the right to be treated equally as an equal human being.

2. I have the right to be whatever my perceived role or status is.

3. I have the right to state my needs and ask for what I want.

4. I have the right to define my limits, look after my needs, and say 'No'.

5. I have the right to express my feelings and opinions.

6. I have the right to ask for time to think before I agree, disagree, or make a final decision.

7. I have the right to make my own decisions.

8. I have the right to reconsider and change my mind.

9. I have the right to say, 'I don't understand,' and ask for clarification or help.

10. I have the right to make mistakes without feeling guilty or being made to feel foolish.

11. I have the right to hold my values.

12. I have the right to be listened to when I speak.

13. I have the right to refuse responsibility for other people's problems if I so choose.

14. I have the right to set my own goals in life and strive to fulfil my expectations against the goals and expectations specified for me by others.

15. I have the right to relate to people without being dependent on them for approval.

**Responsibilities about rights**
- I recognise that I have responsibilities as well as rights.
- I give other people the same rights that I give to myself.

## My Rights in the Workplace

1. I have the right to be treated with respect whatever my position or status.

2. I have the right to say 'No' to requests I consider unreasonable or believe I cannot fulfil.

3. I have the right to request extra time to complete a task.

4. I have the right to ask for time to consider a request.

5. I have the right to be consulted on matters that affect me or my staff.

6. I have the right to be heard by my manager, staff, and colleagues.

7. I have the right to make occasional mistakes.

8. I have the right to ask for assistance and advice.

9. I have the right to training and the opportunity to develop existing skills and learn new ones.

10. I have the right to receive credit and acknowledgment for my achievements at work.

11. I have the right to take care of myself and have sick or compassionate leave without feeling guilty or pressured.

12. I have the right to give constructive criticism to staff about performance or behaviour.

13. I have the right to fulfil my potential.

### Responsibilities about rights
- I am responsible for fulfilling my contractual obligations and the duties within my job description.

Identifying your behaviour patterns and the factors involved will help you understand the changes you must make, which is the first step in the change process.

# What You Have Learned in the previous Chapters

In Chapter One, the book explains the difference between assertive, aggressive, and passive communication. It covers the distinct behaviours of each style and how to identify aggressive, passive, and assertive behaviour. This chapter is important because many people confuse aggressive and assertive behaviour and are hesitant to become more assertive due to the fear of being seen as aggressive. As you discovered, there is a significant difference between the two, especially in the manner in which the message is conveyed to the other person. The main idea is to express yourself effectively while being considerate of others' feelings. We also discussed the barriers that can hinder assertiveness, often formed in childhood and adulthood. By the end of this book, I hope you'll feel more at ease letting go of these barriers. Another important aspect of assertiveness is understanding and asserting your rights in both personal and work life. It's crucial to acknowledge that you deserve these rights just as much as anyone else and give yourself the same rights you give others. I have emphasised on several occasions that simply understanding assertiveness is not enough to learn to be assertive. You also need to understand the factors that prevent you from being assertive so that you can overcome them. Additionally, it's important to understand the underlying reasons behind aggressive behaviour. How can you become assertive if you fear your assertiveness will be met with aggressive behaviour? How can you become assertive if you fear conflict? How can you become assertive when you fear losing the person you need to be assertive with? These questions will be addressed later in this book. The book transitions from theory to practical advice, providing the understanding and techniques needed to become assertive in any situation with anyone.

> ✏️ **Complete Activity 2.0**
> **Your Rights**.

Look at the two lists of rights. These are your rights, and you are entitled to them. Put a cross next to the rights you currently deny yourself and a tick against the rights you would benefit most from.

## My Rights as a Person

☐ I have the right to be treated with respect as an equal human being.

☐ I have the right to be whatever my perceived role or status is.

☐ I have the right to state my needs and ask for what I want.

☐ I have the right to define my limits, look after my needs, and say 'No'.

☐ I have the right to express my feelings and opinions.

☐ I have the right to ask for time to think before I agree, disagree, or make a final decision.

☐ I have the right to make my own decisions.

☐ I have the right to reconsider and change my mind.

☐ I have the right to say, 'I don't understand,' and ask for clarification or help.

☐ I have the right to make mistakes without feeling guilty or being made to feel foolish.

☐ I have the right to hold my values.

☐ I have the right to be listened to when I speak.

☐ I have the right to refuse responsibility for other people's problems if I so choose.

☐ I have the right to set my own goals in life and strive to fulfil my expectations against the goals and expectations specified for me by others.

☐ I have the right to relate to people without being dependent on them for approval.

## Responsibilities about rights

- I recognise that I have responsibilities as well as rights.

- I give other people the same rights that I give to myself.

## My Rights in the Workplace

☐ I have the right to be treated with respect whatever my position or status.

☐ I have the right to say 'No' to requests I consider unreasonable or believe I cannot fulfil.

☐ I have the right to ask for extra time to complete a task.

☐ I have the right to ask for time to consider a request.

☐ I have the right to be consulted on matters that affect me or my staff.

☐ I have the right to be heard by my manager, my staff, and my colleagues.

☐ I have the right to make occasional mistakes.

☐ I have the right to ask for assistance and advice.

☐ I have the right to training and the opportunity to develop existing skills and learn new ones.

- ☐ I have the right to receive credit and acknowledgment for my achievements at work.

- ☐ I have the right to take care of myself and have sick leave or compassionate leave without feeling guilty or pressured.

- ☐ I have the right to give constructive criticism to staff about performance or behaviour.

- ☐ I have the right to fulfil my potential.

## Responsibilities about rights

- ☐ I have the responsibility to fulfil my contractual obligations and the duties within my job description.

# 3.

## *What is aggressive and passive behaviour?*

## What Is the Difference Between Assertive, Passive, and Aggressive Behaviour?

In the previous chapter, we learned about assertiveness, our rights in personal and work lives, the benefits of assertiveness for our lives and relationships, and the negative impact of not being assertive on our health and well-being. When people tell you to be more assertive, "stop being too nice, and stand up for yourself", you might think being assertive means being equally aggressive. For passive individuals, doing something that doesn't come naturally is uncomfortable, and they may not know how to do it, which can be daunting. You don't need to be aggressive to assert yourself, even if someone is aggressive towards you. There's a way to stand up to someone without being aggressive and still achieve a positive outcome. Being assertive does not have the same negative impact as aggression; it has the opposite effect. Assertiveness is often misunderstood and wrongly interpreted as aggression. These two behaviours are entirely different but are frequently confused as being the same. There is a significant distinction between assertive and aggressive behaviour."

The difference between aggressive, assertive, and passive responses will be explained in this Chapter.

The first step to becoming more assertive is understanding assertiveness so you are not afraid to use it. How can you practice assertiveness when worried that it might offend or upset someone and possibly make things worse for yourself? This is why it is important to understand the difference between assertive and aggressive communication before learning to be assertive. You need to be comfortable with asserting yourself before being assertive with someone. The next section provides a detailed explanation of the concepts of assertiveness, aggressiveness, and passivity and will assist you in distinguishing between these three types of responses. Understanding the distinctions between assertive and aggressive behaviour should alleviate any concerns you may have had about assertiveness.

## What Is Assertive Behaviour

### Assertive People are:
Direct, Risk-Taking, Equal, Clear, Honest, Challenging, Caring, Spontaneous, Specific, Initiating, Non-judgmental, Self-Aware

### Assertive People:

- Use 'I' Statements and take responsibility for their actions.

- Listen attentively.

- Make requests, ask for favours, and ask for what they want.

- Refuse other's requests if they are too demanding and what they don't want.

- Exercise choice, make decisions.

- Listen to criticism and accept or reject it.

- Accept compliments.

- Acknowledge and praise other people's qualities and achievements.

- Accept that other people have limitations.

- Share positive and negative feelings, opinions, and experiences with others.

- Have a healthy level of self-esteem.

- Enjoy today and set goals for tomorrow.

- Are firm so that their rights are respected.

- Address problems or things that bother them.

- Question rules or traditions that don't make sense or don't seem fair.

- Start, change, or end conversations.

## Assertive People do not:

- Beat around the bush

- Go behind people's backs.

- Bully.

- Call people names.

- Bottle up their feelings.

- Put others down.

- Manipulate.

- Control others.

## What Is Aggressive and Passive Behaviour

Now that you understand an assertion, it is important to recognise the other ways we may respond, starting with aggression. *Aggressiveness* involves standing up for personal rights and expressing thoughts, feelings, and beliefs in a way that is often *forceful*, sometimes *inappropriate*, and may *violate* the rights of others. The typical aim of aggression is to *dominate* and *win*. Winning is achieved by *humiliating, degrading, belittling, or overpowering* others, making them weaker and less able to express their needs and rights. Superiority is established by *violating* the rights of others and maintained through the belief that the person has more rights and personal worth yet fewer responsibilities than others.

Alternatively, ……

*Non-assertion or Passivity* involves *failing* to express *honest feelings, thoughts, and beliefs* and consequently permitting another person to violate or abuse oneself or expressing one's feelings in such an *apologetic, diffident, self-effacing* manner that others can easily disregard them. It shows a *lack of respect* for *one's own needs*. The passive tester allows their rights to be violated in the belief that they have fewer rights and less worth than others. The goal of non-assertion is to *satisfy* others and to *avoid conflict* at any cost.

The **three paragraphs (groups of words) below** give a clear summary of the behavioural differences in each of the typical responses.

**Passive:** *Vague, Inhibited, Self-pitying, Avoidance, Self-putdown, Wanting, Loser, Ineffective, Cowardly, Victim, Powerless, I Don't Mind, Blaming indirectly, Half listen, Put others down (behind their back), Taking indirectly, Emotional bribery, Martyr, Is afraid to speak, Speaks softly, Avoids looking at people, Shows little or no expression, Slouches and withdraws,*

*Isolates self from groups, Agrees with others despite feelings, Values self less than others, Hurts self to avoid hurting others, Does not reach goals and may not know goals, You are okay/I'm not.*

**Aggressive:** *Demanding, Uncompromising, Judgmental, Manipulative, Deceitful, Reacting, Pressuring, Arrogant, Blaming, Refuses to listen, Puts others down to their face, Taking, Hurtful, Pushy, Loud, Winner, Power-over, Disempowering, Interrupts and talks over others, Speaks loudly, Glares and stares at others, Intimidates others with expressions, Stands rigidly crosses arms and invades others Space, Controls groups, Only considers own feelings and/ or demanding of others, Values self more than others, Hurts others to avoid being hurt, Reaches goals but hurt others in the process, I'm okay/ you're not*

**Assertive:** *Uses 'I' Statements, State needs directly, Honest, Accepts blame, Responsible, Respects self and others, Initiating, Forgiving, Effective, Spontaneous, Realist, Power within, Empowering, Speaks openly, Uses a normal conversational tone, Makes good eye contact, Shows expressions that matches the message,*

*Relaxes and adopts an open posture and expressions, Participates in groups, Speaks to the point, Values self, Equal to others, Hurts no one including self, Reaches goals without alienating others, I'm okay/ You're okay*

Everyone at some time has to cope with a problem and there are two basic instinctual responses that people rely on when encountering a problem one learned response, they are *flight* (passivity) and *fight* (aggressive), and *assertiveness* (learned) which is the most appropriate and successful method when solving these problems because it involves *discussing, arguing, and negotiating.* Many mental health and relationship problems are caused by an over-reliance on the two basic instinctual responses, passivity and aggression.

There is a fourth response that is often not talked about: the *passive-aggressive* response. Passive aggression is the indirect expression of hostility, such as sarcasm, stubbornness, procrastination, or deliberate failure to accomplish tasks. It may also refer to a person who projects their aggression onto others and manages their denial by seeing themselves as blameless victims. These people respond in a passive way that can result in an aggressive response when their passive, indirect manipulation to get the desired results does not work or when they are pushed into a corner.

## Why Do People Respond Aggressively?

People who communicate aggressively or passively do so for one reason: fear. Let's start with why people communicate passively. It's simple - they fear conflict. They prefer to pacify any situation to avoid a conflict. This is because they either do not know how to respond to aggressive behaviour assertively, or they do not have the confidence to respond assertively, or both. They believe that standing up for themselves will only worsen the situation and make matters worse. While some situations may warrant a passive response, such as when your life is in real danger or you are at risk of serious harm, in most cases where there is no real threat, it is not necessary. Sometimes, we fear what we expect might happen and not what will happen. For instance, you might anticipate your boss yelling at or criticising you for making a mistake, but they respond appropriately instead. If you have encountered aggressive people in your life, you are more likely to expect others to respond similarly. Keep your guard up when dealing with people in the future due to negative past experiences. This can hinder your ability to be assertive. Assertion may seem ineffective based on past experiences, but that's not entirely true. Assertion doesn't work with aggressive or passive people. The first important thing to understand about assertiveness is that you will only get a positive outcome from being assertive with another assertive person. In other words, you can only reason with the reasonable. Assertiveness is a tool that enables you to build healthy and genuine relationships and rid yourself of toxic relationships. It's a tool that will protect you from being affected by toxic people, but it's not a tool that will change these people. No one has the power to change anyone; only they can change themselves. Your new assertiveness skills will enable you to set the right boundaries for people to respect you, even if they don't want to. The role of assertiveness is to encourage the development of healthy relationships and to rid oneself of toxic ones. This book will teach you the skills to do this.

As children, we often endure abusive behaviour from adults because we are powerless and vulnerable. However, as we grow into adults, we may fail to recognise that we now have the same power as our peers. We continue to react passively, similar to how we did as children, even in our interactions with other adults. We forget that, as adults, we deserve the same rights, respect, and treatment we extend to our peers. We often forget that we no longer have to tolerate abuse from anyone. This brings me to my next point. We don't have to stand there and take it; we can simply walk away from the abuse. We also don't realise that as adults, we have the choice of who we want in our lives. The first step to becoming assertive is to realise that you have the power and the choice to have whomever you want in your life. You have the option to leave a bad situation and not tolerate abuse or disrespect from anyone. However, you cannot change someone who does not want to change. Assertiveness is a skill that allows you to communicate your needs, but it cannot force someone to give you what you need if they are unwilling. A healthy relationship is about give and take, not just one person giving and receiving nothing in return. Sometimes, it's better to walk away from an unhealthy situation that you cannot change but need to change to be happy rather than just tolerating it and being unhappy. The people in your life will either be good for you or not. You have the right and the choice to keep them in your life or not. Being assertive allows you to filter your relationships. Only genuine people will respond to your assertiveness. Those who don't are the ones who only want to take from you and give you little back. Once you become assertive, you can distinguish the 'genuine' people in your life from the 'toxic' ones.

    Some people communicate passively to avoid conflicts they feel they cannot escape. When passive, they ignore negative and hurtful comments, let others dominate them, and tolerate hurtful behaviour. They believe that walking away would only worsen the situation. Many aggressive individuals are aware of the potential consequences of their actions, such as losing their jobs or facing legal charges. In most cases, the fear of facing aggression is often unfounded, as aggressive individuals are likelier to make threats than act on them. To become more assertive, it's important to recognise that aggressive people understand the limits of their behaviour and the potential consequences. You also have the right to walk away from a situation rather than tolerate someone else's aggression.

We will discuss how to deal with an aggressive person later in the book…

Assertive individuals surround themselves with like-minded, confident, and well-adjusted people. They avoid those who may endanger their well-being. If being assertive does not change a situation, the only option is to remove oneself. For example, if you cannot address your boss's negative behaviour towards you assertively, your best recourse may be to find a more positive and healthier workplace. There are reasons why people may communicate passively other than fear of conflict. One reason is not believing they deserve to be treated the right way. Low self-esteem is probably the most common reason for passive communication. When you have low self-esteem, you may believe that you are inferior to others. If you believe this, you are highly likely to assume that anyone who challenges you is right and that you are wrong, regardless of the situation. When you automatically blame yourself, you will likely overlook evidence and find it more difficult to assert yourself. How can you resolve a situation assertively when you don't even know if you are right or wrong? And how can you determine right or wrong when you don't consider the available facts? It's crucial for people with low self-esteem to base their conclusions on facts rather than assumptions. Assertiveness involves presenting facts in a positive manner to achieve a desirable outcome. Healthy self-esteem is essential for assertiveness because being treated with respect, fairness, and appropriateness contributes to feeling valued and building self-worth. Therefore, assertiveness is important for maintaining healthy self-esteem and learning to be assertive can also help improve self-esteem. Developing self-esteem to feel more comfortable and confident in using assertive skills is beneficial.

It's important to have healthy self-esteem to assert yourself, and being assertive is crucial for maintaining healthy self-esteem. If you lack a healthy sense of self-worth, learning to be assertive can also help. Developing your self-esteem will also greatly benefit you by making you feel more comfortable and confident in using your new assertive skills.

## Aggressive people lack self-esteem

Did you know that most people who are aggressive also have low self-esteem? Aggression is often mistaken for confidence, but it is usually a sign of poor self-esteem. Aggressive behaviour is sometimes perceived as confidence because it may seem brave to abuse someone verbally, but in reality, aggressive people often target passive individuals. You rarely see aggressive people confronting someone who is likely to stand up to them. You may have noticed this pattern if you remember your school days. The bully always targeted students who didn't stand up for themselves. Have you ever noticed a bully challenging someone who is likely to stand up to them? The bully earns respect by intimidating and instilling fear in others. By targeting someone unlikely to fight back, the bully ensures a victory and achieves their goal of intimidation and gaining respect, even if it's only based on fear. Unfortunately, the victim doesn't realise that they are feeding the bully's ego and hiding the bully's insecurities by responding passively.

It's unfortunate that bullies often continue their behaviour into adulthood. They tend to surround themselves with people they can manipulate, control, and intimidate in their personal and professional lives. This behaviour helps them maintain a false sense of self-confidence, as they are used to getting what they want without any opposition or disagreement. Aggressive individuals will only show respect towards assertive individuals because they are compelled to do so. An assertive person is not daunted by aggression, which puts the aggressive individual in an uncomfortable position since they are accustomed to being in control and getting their way without resistance. An assertive person will confront an aggressive individual in a suitable, respectful, and tactful manner, focusing solely on the facts. They prefer not to get involved in a conflict they know will lead to nothing. Instead, they like to discuss the problem and negotiate a solution. They expect the other person to accept blame where it is due and to present their facts in the argument. They want a win-win outcome. An aggressive person does not know how to play this way. They are used to bullying their way to achieve one thing: to win. Aggressive people do not like to lose; when dealing with an assertive person, there is always the chance of not winning, depending on the facts presented in the argument.

Aggressive individuals tend to surround themselves with passive people who agree with and accommodate them. In the workplace, you can observe how an aggressive, manipulative, and controlling manager treats assertive employees with respect while treating those who do not assert themselves unfairly and disrespectfully. This is because they are intimidated by assertive individuals but not by passive ones. In their personal lives, aggressive individuals will similarly treat assertive family members with respect while not extending the same treatment to those who do not assert themselves. Unfortunately, this is often the case.

So, what causes someone to become aggressive? It's often linked to low self-esteem. Some people develop unhealthy coping mechanisms such as over-pleasing, accommodating, and avoidance to avoid rejection by others. The more they are accepted and the less they are rejected, the more valued they feel, even if it means sacrificing their own needs. Aggressive individuals often resort to unhealthy coping mechanisms such as manipulation, dominance, put-downs, and intimidation to create a false sense of respect for themselves, compensating for their lack of self-esteem. The more people they can control, the more powerful and superior they feel. It is a misconception that aggressive people are confident. Unfortunately, aggression is a learned behaviour that can develop from childhood. When a child is raised in a hostile and aggressive environment, they may grow up to be either aggressive or passive. The behaviour they adopt in adulthood largely depends on the child's upbringing and what worked for them to avoid harm. A child may have avoided punishment and harm by accommodating and not "rocking the boat," and this behaviour will likely continue into adulthood. Conversely, if aggression was more effective in their childhood, they are likely to continue using aggression in adulthood.

Children raised in a household where they were privileged to see their family members discuss and assertively resolve issues are also more likely to continue this form of communication in adult life.

The message I want to convey from this section of the book is that aggressive people may seem confident and intimidating but lack assertive communication skills. They use aggression to assert their dominance and boost their low self-worth. If they had strong self-esteem, they wouldn't need to be aggressive. Aggressive people are insecure and use aggression to hide their insecurities. They target you because they've gotten away with it before and expect to continue doing so. When you learn to be assertive and use your new skills with them, you'll notice a positive change in their behaviour towards you.

## Why Do People Respond in a Passive Way?

Our upbringing and the guidance we received during our childhood have significantly influenced our behaviour and communication as adults. We often mimic the behaviour of those who impacted us most during our formative years. For instance, if a parent handled situations aggressively, we might adopt an aggressive, passive, or passive-aggressive approach as adults rather than being assertive. This is because we may not have been taught how to be assertive. Our experiences also shape our approach. If being aggressive has resulted in positive outcomes in the past, we are likely to continue using this communication style, even if it's not the most effective way to handle situations. While aggression can effectively get what you want from passive individuals, it often fails when used with other aggressive or assertive people. The problem with aggressive behaviour is that it can exacerbate the situation you're trying to address and even lead to conflict.

Responding passively to situations avoids conflict, even if it means giving in, accommodating, taking full blame (even when it is not deserved), or disregarding your feelings. This approach allows the other person to "win" even when they are in the wrong. When handling situations passively, it may seem like you're keeping the peace, but in reality, it often results in a 'win-lose' situation where the other person always wins and you always lose. Avoiding conflict in the short term can lead to serious damage in the long term, impacting your happiness and mental and physical health.

## Using a Passive Communication Style for Fear of Conflict

The main reason people handle situations passively is to avoid conflict. People who fear conflict usually grew up around it and may have experienced abusive or punitive parenting. For many, even hearing someone raise their voice can trigger anxiety and bring back past trauma. Coming from a dysfunctional background as a child, you may have felt vulnerable and had little control. As an adult, it's important to remember that you have the power to decide who you want in your life and how you want to be treated. Even if there are still people in your life who mistreat you, it's essential to recognise that you are no longer a vulnerable child with no choice, rights, or control. You have the option to walk away from someone who is being aggressive towards you. You can also choose to leave a toxic relationship, whether it is personal or professional. As a child, you may not always have these same choices.

In an adult-to-adult relationship, both parties know their rights and the civil laws that protect them. As adults, we understand the laws against assaulting and physically harming someone, as well as the workplace policies against bullying and emotional, verbal, and physical abuse. We are also fully aware of the consequences of not following these rules, such as losing jobs, being sued, or facing demotion or performance management. Unless you are involved in a domestic violent situation where there is a high risk of being harmed, any other fear you might have is likely to be unrealistic and based solely on insecurities stemming from negative experiences in your past.

In every situation where you need to be assertive, ask yourself, "What is the likelihood of the person going against company rules or legal regulations?" and "What consequences would they face if they were to cross these boundaries?" Everyone knows how far they can go before facing consequences. This is why most aggressive people only go as far as you allow.

## Crossing Boundaries in a Personal Relationship

Even though aggressive people are aware of the consequences of crossing personal boundaries in their relationships, they still do it. Why? Because they believe they can get away with it. It's easier for them to disregard boundaries in personal relationships than in professional ones. Their aggressive behaviour is harder to hide in their professional life, making the consequences more likely. The support for the other person in their professional life is more readily available. However, not respecting relationship boundaries in their personal life is likely to lead to the termination of the relationship. If someone doesn't want to lose you, they will likely accept and respect your boundaries. Sometimes, a person may have been allowed to get away with bad behaviour, but it doesn't mean the relationship isn't genuine. Being assertive can help you determine the genuineness of your relationships. Sometimes it's better to end a relationship that undermines your self-esteem and health and prevents you from being happy. Everyone deserves respect, but not everyone is willing to earn it. If you don't receive the respect you deserve, you may need to end the relationship to stop feeling disrespected. You have a duty to care for others and yourself.

You cannot force someone to treat you the right way if they don't want to, but you can choose whether or not to tolerate abuse, aggression, and disrespect. If most people treat you well and consider your needs and feelings, then it's not you who's the problem. Some people will always respect you and do the right thing, while others take advantage of those they know will allow it. Being passive and non-assertive is a choice that can be changed, not a fixed trait. You don't need to fear conflict when you have the choice to engage in it or not. You can walk away when a discussion or argument becomes heated. You have the right to be respected and to remove yourself from abusive situations. Non-assertive people may forget they have the right to be respected and treated well. To be able to walk away from conflict, they need to stop fearing it. Assertive people don't fear conflict because they understand the boundaries of acceptable behaviour in society. They know that walking away from an aggressive situation won't escalate it. There's a difference between avoiding a conflict and choosing not to engage in one.

When you avoid a conflict by giving in or just taking the aggression from the other person, you are giving away your power to that person. This will only make matters worse for you in the long run. When you walk away from conflict, you choose to hold onto your power and ask the other person to respect you. There is nothing more humiliating for an aggressive person than to be put in a powerless position. What better way to create this than to show them you are not intimidated by them by 'walking away' from the situation? When you do this, you are telling them to 'grow up' (after all, we're no longer in kindergarten), and that if they want to address an issue with you, they will need to do it correctly!

When you exercise your new assertiveness skills, you will be able to handle any situation and gain respect in both your personal and professional life. The rest of the book will teach you how to assert yourself at work with your co-workers, superiors, subordinates, customers/clients, and your personal life with your partner, children, siblings, friends, and family. To be assertive, it's important to learn assertiveness skills and not be afraid to use them. One of the most challenging aspects is using assertiveness skills with aggressive people. Some individuals find it more difficult to assert themselves in their personal lives than in their professional lives, or vice versa. In personal relationships, the fear of losing the person may be the biggest obstacle, while in professional settings, the fear of losing one's job is a common concern.

However, people often overcome their fears when they realise that their fears are unrealistic and that the "worst case" scenario is unlikely to occur. They also understand that what they fear losing may not be worth holding onto. For instance, if standing up to a disrespectful boss leads to losing a job, the individual may not have lost much. In this scenario, staying in the job would probably cause increased stress, harm mental health, and damage self-esteem. It's crucial to understand that someone who doesn't respect you should not be a part of your life and will only bring you pain. Ultimately, any personal or professional relationship in which you are merely surviving rather than thriving is not worth keeping. Surrounding yourself with the right people can lead to personal and professional growth while being around the wrong people can lead to ongoing struggle and inhibition.

## Crossing Boundaries in a Professional Relationship

In the workplace, many people struggle with being assertive. They find it challenging to assert themselves with colleagues, customers, staff, and managers. Some may find it easier to be assertive with their staff but not with their supervisors, while others may find it easier with colleagues but not with their staff. This difficulty often depends on what they fear losing, such as their job, boss' respect, likability, acceptance, or face value. It's crucial to recognise the role assertiveness plays in shaping relationships. Being assertive can help reveal hidden agendas, manipulation, and toxic behaviour in people. By identifying these behaviours, you can better protect yourself and your self-esteem.

How often have you witnessed someone in your workplace losing control of their behaviour while addressing an issue with someone? Probably never. How frequently have you observed a colleague, subordinate, or supervisor losing control of their behaviour throughout your career? Probably never. This is because the people you work with understand the boundaries they must respect to keep their job, avoid a bullying/harassment case, or prevent a legal claim against them. They may test these boundaries, but rarely do they push beyond them because they know the consequences they would face. As an employee, you are protected by the rules and guidelines set by Fair Work and your company's Policies and Procedures. Employers must ensure that their workplace provides a safe environment to work in. An employer who crosses these health and safety boundaries risks losing their job and facing serious consequences. And they are aware of this. Understanding your rights as an employee and the company's policies and procedures is crucial when exercising your assertiveness skills and dealing with aggressive individuals. Being aware of the protection provided by workplace rules can make it easier to assert yourself. In the upcoming sections of the book, you will learn what to say, how to respond, and when to respond to an aggressive supervisor, subordinate, colleague, or customer in a manner that garners the same respect as assertive individuals. The practical part of the book will present common scenarios that you can relate to and use to learn how to handle them assertively.

## Using a passive communication style due to fear of rejection.

We just discussed how and why people react aggressively in certain situations. Now, let's explore why people may respond passively. While passive and non-assertive behaviour can help avoid conflicts and disharmony in relationships, it does little to foster healthy and meaningful connections. Constantly trying to please and overcommitting may maintain stability and peace in relationships, especially when the other person doesn't have to compromise much and mostly gets their way. However, this approach does not contribute to your well-being and happiness. Passive and non-assertive individuals tend to avoid confrontation because they fear rejection. They would rather endure feelings of not being valued, appreciated, or respected than face rejection. This is because they interpret rejection as a sign of not being good enough for the other person, rather than realising that they were rejected because they didn't constantly cater to the other person's ego by always trying to please them or giving in to their demands. In other words, they believe they were rejected because they didn't provide what the other person wanted, not because they weren't good enough. If you recall the last time someone rejected you, consider whether it was due to personal criticism or if they rejected you because you no longer met their expectations. Keep in mind that rejection often comes from toxic people who don't appreciate, respect, or value you. In the long run, being rejected by such individuals is actually a favour. Assertiveness helps you distinguish between people who support you and those who don't. The more assertive you are, the more you'll attract the right people and remove those who don't deserve a place in your life.

## How Assertiveness Can Help Prevent Getting Involved in an Abusive Relationship.

In the first three months of a relationship, seeing someone's true colours is difficult. Rather, you may catch glimpses of the real person. It's been observed that aggressive individuals often struggle with low self-esteem. Even though the abuser in an abusive relationship may come across as confident, deep down, they suffer from critically low self-esteem. Their self-esteem is dependent on controlling, manipulating, and intimidating their victim. On the other hand, the victim of an abusive relationship may initially enter the relationship feeling confident and independent. However, as time passes, they may experience criticism, verbal abuse, manipulation, and control from their abusive partner, leading to a loss of confidence. As the abuser gains more power, control, and confidence, they may become increasingly aggressive and violent. Consequently, the victim may become more passive, accommodating, and powerless, doing anything to avoid harm.

It's important to gather as much information as possible about a person in the first few weeks of meeting them before becoming too emotionally involved. Ignoring issues early in the relationship, no matter how minor they may seem, can hinder obtaining important information about the person you're involved with. In the initial phase of meeting someone, it is common for both parties to try to impress each other and to hide their weaknesses. This is when being assertive can be really helpful. By addressing something, even if it's minor, in an assertive way, you will see how the person responds. The way a person responds to your assertive message will tell you a lot about how they deal with constructive criticism, whether they are passive, aggressive, or assertive communicators, how they accept responsibility for their actions if they respect people, how they deal with a stressful situation, and if they react to situations in an appropriate, 'normal' way.

When you confidently address someone's behaviour, you can determine if the person you're getting involved with is genuine, confident, well-adjusted, and a good communicator. It's easier to end a relationship early on when you're not too emotionally invested rather than later when you are. Assertiveness is a powerful tool for evaluating the quality of a relationship and avoiding getting into an abusive one.

Now that you understand the meanings of being assertive, passive, passive-aggressive, and aggressive and why people can become aggressive, you can learn how to assert yourself in any situation, even when dealing with an aggressive person.

##  Activity 3.0 – An Assessment of My Behaviour

Circle the characteristics in each of the categories (groups of words) that you believe you possess.

**Passive:** Vague, Subservient, Inhibited, Self-pitying, Avoidance, Put self-down, Wanting, Loser, Ineffectual, Cowardly, Victim, Powerless, I don't mind

**Aggressive:** Demanding, Uncompromising, Arrogant, Blaming, Refuse to listen, Put others down, Taking, Hurtful, Pushy, Loud, Winner, Power over, Disempowering

**Indirect:** Judgmental, Manipulative, Deceitful, Blaming Indirectly, Half listen, Put others down, Talking indirectly, Reacting, Pressuring, Emotional bribery, Martyr, Powerless, I don't mind

**Assertive:** Use 'I' statements, States needs directly, Honest, Accept Blame, Responsible, Respect self and others, Initiating, Forgiving, Effective, Spontaneous, Realist, Power with him, Empowering

# 4.

## *How to Become Assertive*

An important step before learning assertiveness skills is to know your personal/workplace rights. If you do not know these rights, you will find it difficult to assert yourself with someone. The reason for this is that before you can set a boundary with someone, or be able to address an issue with them, you need to know whether you are in the right or wrong. How can you address the issue regarding the unfair pay that your boss is giving you when you don't know if you have the right to the pay you think you deserve? How can you address the problem that your boss has with you regarding the mistakes that you have been making when you don't know that you have the right to make the occasional mistake and that you have the right to receive the training that he promised to give you when you first started?

## Your Personal / Workplace Rights

As previously covered in the Personal and Workplace Rights section, it is extremely difficult to be assertive with someone if you do not know where you stand on the issue that you want to discuss and if you don't know if you are right. There will be some people that you will need to be assertive with, who will use manipulation to twist things around to make you feel as though you do not have the right to question, ask for, or discuss an issue that you need to address that is impacting on you, and not them. You don't want to leave a discussion feeling worse, guilty, and blamed for something unjustified. All that will do is reinforce to you that misconception that assertiveness does not work, when in fact it is because you do not know your right.

Manipulation is a tactic commonly used to shift blame towards the other person, and for them to escape the change you are asking them to make. Whether you are being assertive with someone in your personal life or your workplace, if you are aware of your rights before engaging in an assertive discussion and are prepared for manipulation, you will have a stronger chance to push your message across. You are less likely to get caught in the manipulation. Later in the book, you will learn how not to fall victim to manipulation. Refer back to the Personal and Workplace Rights section if you need to.

## Assertive Behaviour and Body Language

You can have the 'best' assertive message, but without delivering it accompanied by assertive behaviour, it will not be as effective. Demonstrating confidence through body language is so important when being assertive. If you show any signs of confusion, lack of confidence, uncertainty, vulnerability, or doubt, then your chances of success at being assertive will be low. A manipulator will rely on your body language and behaviour to spot any weaknesses and gauge their chance of successfully manipulating you. An assertive person who delivers their message along with assertive behaviour will incapacitate the manipulator. You must understand that manipulators do not like to lose or be put in a situation that will highlight their insecurities and vulnerabilities. So, if they sense that you are a strong and confident person and your assertive message is clear and concise, they are less likely to attempt to manipulate you. In some cases, where someone has become used to getting their way with you, it may take some time to accept the new assertive you. But when you persist, stand your ground, and consistently assertively deliver your assertive message, they will eventually accept the new assertive you.

The key is not to give up just because it does not work straight away, and if after several attempts you cannot break through the wall, then you will have no choice but to accept that the person does not want to change or is not able to change. Sometimes it's not that people do not want to change the way you need them to for the relationship. Still, it's because there are underlying issues that you might not be aware of until you repeatedly apply your assertion to highlight these issues. Nevertheless, it is still their responsibility to at least seek professional help to address their issues and to have a healthy relationship with you.

Below are the eight assertive behaviours that need to accompany your assertive message.

## The Eight Assertive Behaviour

1. Know what you want to say: You won't appear confident if you are unsure of what you want. You could appear foolish by asking for something you eventually realise is not what you want. Know what you want to change, the problem, the solution, the options available, and the causal factors.

2. Say it: Don't hesitate or beat around the bush; come right out with it. Practice before you say it and check for appropriateness.

3. Be specific: Say exactly what you want or don't want so there can be no confusion. Begin with the word 'I'. No long explanations are necessary.

4. Say it as soon as possible: Do not let too much time pass, as this builds up apprehension. On the other hand, do not say it at the peak of your anger. Wait for your anger to pass. Remember, emotions can cloud logic.

5. Look the person in the eye: People feel more comfortable if you look directly at them. You look shifty if you cannot look them in the eye. You certainly will not come across as someone who knows what they want and is confident

enough to get it. Eye contact is the first sign of confidence or lack of confidence. Practice in the mirror or on someone that you are more comfortable with.

6. Look relaxed: You will convey anxiety by shifting from one foot to another, waving your arms around, or conversely being too rigid. Practising your message beforehand will allow it to flow more naturally. Taking deep, slow breaths 15-20mins before and during will help keep you calm and focused.

7. Avoid laughing nervously: Smile if it's appropriate, but if you giggle or laugh you won't look as if you mean what you say. This will confuse the person you are speaking to. Again, practice makes perfect.

8. Don't whine or be sarcastic: Be direct and honest. Whining and pleading can either annoy the person or make them feel guilty. That is being manipulative. On the other hand, being sarcastic communicates hostility as you put the other person down.

## The Assertive Formula
**Basic Assertiveness**

Most assertiveness books focus on teaching you a specific assertive technique/response for every situation. You might come away from reading these books with a bag of tricks, but it can be difficult to remember which trick to use for each situation. I have developed a 5–Step Formula that can be applied to any situation. You don't need to learn and memorise several techniques or when to use them to be assertive. All you will need to store in your memory is one formula.

The formula has five levels of communication, each serving a vital purpose in communicating your needs. The scenario below will demonstrate how the formula works.

*"A work colleague has left the organisation, and his/her work responsibilities have been handed over to you to manage in addition to your job role responsibilities. As a result, you have become very stressed and tired as you have had to increase your work pace and work hours to complete the responsibilities of both roles."*

Before applying the 5-Step Formula, you must also apply three steps to prepare your assertive message. Preparing the message that you want to deliver will make it flow more easily, keep your voice steady, and keep your message on track.

**Step 1:** You need to identify your need, e.g., to reduce your workload back to that outlined in your normal position description/work contract.

**Step 2:** You need to accept that you have the right to meet that need. Your employer has a duty of care towards you and a responsibility to provide a safe work environment.

**Step 3:** Work out the script (your assertive message) that you will use to communicate across the change/s that you need using the formula below

Let's use the above scenario to demonstrate the 5-Step Formula below:

# THE 5 STEP ASSERTIVENESS FORMULA:

## Level 1: Start with a Positive Comment

To prevent the other person from becoming defensive.

e.g. *"I enjoy working here, and I love my job, but...."*

## Level 2: Give a Clear Explanation of the Problem

To prevent confusion of what needs to change/what the problem/issue is.

e.g. *"Ever since Mary left, my workload has increased and..."*

## Level 3: Explain how the Problem is Affecting you Emotionally/Physically

To ensure the person understands the severity of the problem and why you need to bring it to their attention.

e.g. *"....I feel very stressed/resentful/taken for granted etc."*

## Level 4: Consequence or Loss to the Person if the Problem Continued

To Ensure that Change Happens. Change will only occur if the problem continues and it was impacting on the person who is responsible for resolving the problem.

e.g. *".... I'm bringing this to your attention because I like my job but cannot continue feeling this stressed".*

## Level 5: Negotiation of a Solution

To achieve a win-win situation.

e.g. If your employer explains that he has no one else to do these extra responsibilities and promises to fill the position as soon as possible, and asks you to continue to cover both roles, it is still his problem to resolve, not yours. Your responsibility is to meet the expected standards within your position, which you are being paid to do, not the other position.

Negotiation: In this case, you might suggest that a percentage of your normal role, or of the one to be filled, be delegated to other staff to ease the burden and stress and that you can only assist for another couple of weeks. This will encourage your employer to act quickly on resolving this matter and to take the matter seriously – given that it is now impacting on him/her.

## Starting with a Positive Comment

Starting your assertive message with a positive comment will help to minimise the risk of the person putting their guard up and becoming defensive which can get in the way of getting your full message across. Some people do not take well to being told that they are doing the wrong thing or that you are upset with them. Briefly sharing one or two positive aspects of your relationship or the person with them, and not just bringing up negatives can be an effective technique, especially in encouraging active listening.

## Giving a Clear Explanation of the Problem

To be able to work out a solution, you need to have a clear understanding of what the problem is, and what is causing the problem. In the previous scenario example, the problem was 'overworking and over-committing'; the solution was to reduce the workload by delegating it to other staff members. By first understanding the problem, you will be able to communicate it. It's not enough to convey how the problem is making you feel 'stressed or tired'; you also need to explain what is causing you to feel this way. Simply informing your employer that you are feeling stressed and not coping might give you a little sympathy but might not give you the necessary changes you need to feel better. So, once you identify the cause of the problem, only then will you be able to find the solution needed to address it.

## Explaining how the Problem is Impacting on You

Using the scenario example above, you might be concerned that letting your employer know that you are struggling to cope with the workload is going to go against you, but an employer who uses this against you and shows no empathy, knowing your proven track record of previously coping and of your performance to date, is a clear indication of a nongenuine employer, and possibly toxic workplace. Given the circumstances, you have the right to feel what you are meant to feel. Your employer would be experiencing similar feelings and symptoms if their workload had increased. Don't feel embarrassed or guilty for feeling what anyone would feel under similar circumstances. Don't accept someone's judgment of you when they haven't experienced the same. Anyone who ignores the obvious facts you present to them is trying to manipulate you into accepting the situation for their convenience and benefit. Your health and well-being are more important than that.

## Giving a Consequence

Again, using the scenario example of your employer giving you too much work. People will change a situation only when they are being impacted by it. If you point out to your employer, the problem, the cause, and how it is impacting you, you might receive sympathy from them, but you are not guaranteed to get the change that you need, or at least not immediately unless the consequence you give will have a direct impact on them. By consequence, I mean pointing out the negative impact the situation will have on them if they do not change it. If you want change to happen, it has to have a negative effect on your employer; otherwise, resolving the problem will not be a priority. Ensure to give the employer a glimpse of the potential impact that ignoring the problem might have on them directly. For instance, losing you, an important asset to the organization, could be a potential consequence. Of course, you should not threaten them as this would be aggressive. Instead, you would point out to them that you can no longer sustain this workload, and that for your health and well-being, you will have no choice but to seek alternative employment if the situation is not resolved soon. What impact do you think this will have on them and the organisation if they lose a valuable employee, who is a great asset to the organisation? Again, if your employer does not demonstrate empathy and a duty of care towards you, you are best to seek alternative employment with an employer who does. And, if you are not in a financial position to follow through with the consequences, start looking for something else while you continue working there. There is no point in giving someone a consequence if you are not prepared to follow through with it.

## Negotiating a Solution

Not every situation will need this step. The problem is resolvable in many situations, but the solution is not implemented. That is, people tolerate the problem and do not assert themselves for the problem to be resolved. Negotiations usually take place when the solution presented is not easy to implement. For example, what if your employer has advertised to fill that position and no one applied for it? What if the position required specialised skills that weren't as easy to find? Then what? While the ideal solution might not always be possible, a temporary solution might be in the interim. They might be able to hire temporary staff to take on the more mundane and basic tasks you are performing, allowing you to focus more on the more responsible/ complex tasks. Or there might be enough staff to spread the workload amongst. When negotiating a solution, the goal is to achieve a win-win outcome. Just because the obvious solution does not work, does not mean that no other options are available. It's always a good idea for you to work out all possible options before presenting your case to someone, as this will increase your chances of achieving a positive outcome.

> ✏ **Activity 4.0 – Apply the 5 Step Assertiveness Formula**
>
> Apply the formula to the following scenarios.

Apply the formula to the following scenarios. Come up with your own responses based on the formula i.e. *1. Positive Comment, 2. Problem, 3. How the problem is affecting you, 4. Consequences, 5. Negotiation (if needed).*

1. You are watching a movie, and the people seated in front of you are making it hard to hear the movie.

2. At a work meeting, one of your colleagues is constantly interrupting you when you are speaking.

3. You'd like to ask your boss for a pay rise .

4. You spoke with your boss about an idea you have to improve the efficiency of a system at work. He tells you it's a great idea and he will ask one of your work colleagues to do the job. But you want to do the job yourself.

5. You are looking forward to a quiet night alone, and a relative calls you and asks you to babysit.

6. Your parents/ in-laws call and tell you that they will be dropping by. You are busy.

7. Two of your employees are wasting time chatting, and the work is piling up, adding pressure to other employees who are complaining to you. You are their supervisor.

8. A good friend is always late for plans you made together. You have not said anything for several weeks.

9. A date and time for a meeting has been set. You are committed elsewhere, though, and cannot make that time. This meeting is important for you to attend.

10. Your partner works the same hours outside of the home that you do. They are not contributing to the household chores.


In this chapter, you learned that you don't need a bag of techniques or scripts to assert yourself in different situations. All you need is the 5-Step Assertive Formula that can be applied in both your personal and professional life, and with anyone, and for any problem. We applied the formula to several commonly experienced scenarios to demonstrate how useful and easy it is. Later on, the 5-Step Formula will be applied to some of the most common scenarios experienced in our personal lives, such as children, partners, family, and friends, and in our work lives, such as customers, co-workers, supervisors, and staff.

# 5.

## *Applying the Assertive Formula*

We will now use some typical scenarios to demonstrate how you would use the 5-Step Assertive Formula to resolve these situations assertively.

**1. You are at XYZ Burger Cafe and order your favourite burger with mayonnaise instead of their 'Special Sauce', but they give you one with the wrong sauce. This isn't the first time that they have gotten your order wrong. In a calm tone, you would say:**

**Level 1:** Start with a Positive Comment.

Ask to speak to the Store Manager.

What you would say to the Store Manager:

*"I have been a long-term and regular customer..."*


**Level 2:** Give a clear explanation of the problem/issue.

*"And have had a few orders in the past that were incorrect..."*


**Level 3:** Explain how the problem is affecting you emotionally/physically.

"Each time I have received an incorrect order, I have had to return it to your store. This is very inconvenient and a waste of my time. As the store manager, you are responsible for ensuring that your staff are properly trained to provide quality service to your customers."


**Level 4:** Consequence or loss to the person if the

problem continues.

> "If this problem is not addressed and I continue to be inconvenienced by inaccurate orders, then I will need to write to a letter of complaint about this Store to your Head Office/Corporate Office."

**2. You are in a queue waiting in line to be served. Suddenly, someone cuts in front of you. In a calm tone, you would say:**

**Level 1:** Start with a Positive Comment.
(No need to give a positive comment in this case)

**Level 2:** Give a clear explanation of the problem/issue.

> *"Excuse me, I have been waiting in the queue for 15 minutes, and you jumped in front of me."*

**Level 3:** Explain how the problem is affecting you emotionally/physically.

Point to the end of the queue: *"The end of the queue is over there"*

**Level 4:** Consequence or loss to the person if the problem continues.

*"I would suggest that you go to the end of the queue so that you do not upset other people who have also been waiting for a while".*

**3. After leaving a store where you purchased some items, you discover you were short-changed. In a calm tone, you would say:**

**Level 1:** Start with a Positive Comment.

*"Excuse me, this has never happened to me before in this store, but you have given me the wrong change"*

**Level 2:** Give a clear explanation of the problem/issue.

*"I gave you a $50 note, and here is my receipt"*

**Level 3:** Explain how the problem is affecting you emotionally/physically.

(In this situation, this level would only be needed if the retail assistant refused to give you the correct change even if you had evidence to prove they were wrong. In that case, you would then be best to ask for the Store Manager). If you have evidence to prove your case, getting the correct change back shouldn't be a problem.


**Level 4:** Consequence or loss to the person if the problem continues.

(This level would only be used if the Store Manager refused to give you back your correct change, even though you had evidence to prove it). In that case, you would inform the Store Manager of the consequences they would incur if they did not correct their error.

In a calm tone, you would say, *"I have given you proof that I have been given the wrong change, and I am sure that you have security footage that will prove that I gave your assistant a $50 note; if* *you do not give me the correct change I will make a formal complaint to Consumer Affairs."*

**4. It's your day off, and you are behind on an assignment you must complete for your course by tomorrow when your parent/ roommate/ partner comes in and asks you to do a favour for them that could wait. In a calm tone, you would say:**

**Level 1:** Start with a Positive Comment.
*"You know I am always happy to do you a favour"*

**Level 2:** Give a clear explanation of the problem/issue.
*"But I am in the middle of an assignment due tomorrow."*

*"Seeing that it's not urgent, I am happy to do it (the following day/s)"*

**Level 3:** Explain how the problem is affecting you emotionally/physically.

*"If I don't use this time to complete my assignment, I won't do a good job of it, and rushing it will cause me stress".*

**Level 4:** Consequence or loss to the person if the problem continues.

If the person persists, stand your ground, and say:

*"Look I don't want to resent you if I get a poor mark for my assignment. I will help you (reinforce the time/date you will be able to do the favour).*


**5. A friend drops in for a visit, and they stay too long, and you have an important task to finish by the end of the day that you may not have enough time to complete. In a calm tone, you would say:**

**Level 1:** Start with a Positive Comment.

*"As always, I have really enjoyed your company and had a great morning/ afternoon…"*

**Level 2:** Give a clear explanation of the

problem/issue.

*"I would hate to cut our time short, but I have an important job to finish by the end of the day."*

**Level 3:** Explain how the problem is affecting you emotionally/physically.

*"If I don't complete it by the end of the day my boss will not be happy with me if I do not have something to present to the meeting tomorrow."*

**Level 4:** Consequence or loss to the person if the problem continues.

You would only need to use this level if your friend persists. In this case, you would say:

*"I'm sorry, but I need that time; I'll see you again."*

If they refuse to leave:

*"I've asked you nicely to leave for good reason; as a good friend, I expect you to understand. There have been many times when I have respectfully*

*done the right thing by you, and as a good friend, I would like you to do the same for me."*


**6. You ask for a Latte; however, they give you a Cappuccino instead by mistake. In a calm tone, you would say:**

**Level 1:** Start with a Positive Comment.

*"I'm not sure if you heard me clearly, but...*


**Level 2:** Give a clear explanation of the problem/ issue.

*"I asked for a Latte, not a Cappuccino. Can you please give me a Latte instead? Thank you."*


**Level 3:** Explain how the problem is affecting you emotionally/ physically.
(This level is not needed in this case)

**Level 4:** Consequence or loss to the person if the problem continues.
(This level is not needed in this case)

**7. It has been brought to your attention that one of your colleagues is ruminating about you. In a calm tone, you would say:**

**Level 1:** Start with a Positive Comment.

*"I always thought that you were trustworthy and that we had a good working relationship, however ...."*

**Level 2: Give a clear explanation of the problem/ issue.**

*"I was informed by a work colleague that you have been spreading the rumour (give details). Is that true?"*

**Level 3:** Explain how the problem is affecting you emotionally/ physically.

If the colleague admits to spreading the rumour:

> *"I don't appreciate that you go behind my back and spread nasty rumours about me that are not true".*

If the colleague denies the rumour and you have evidence supporting the accusation:

> *"I know that the source is trustworthy, and they would not have informed me of it if it wasn't true. I don't appreciate that you go behind my back and spread nasty rumours about me that are not true"*

**Level 4:** Consequence or loss to the person if the problem continues.

If the colleague admits to spreading the rumour:

> *"If you do not stop spreading this rumour, I have no choice but to report it to (manager's name). And in the future, if you have an issue with me, I would appreciate it if you would do the decent thing and speak to me about it rather than going behind my back "*

If the colleague denies the rumour and you have evidence supporting the accusation: (repeat the same consequence as above).

> *"If you do not stop spreading this rumour, I have no choice but to report it to (manager's name). And in the future, if you have an issue with me, I would appreciate it if you did the decent thing and spoke to me about it rather than go behind my back".*

**8. You are given a written quote for repairs on your computer. But later, when you pick it up, you are billed for additional work and an amount higher than quoted. You weren't given a call to inform you of the additional work needed and the extra costs you would need to pay if you decided to proceed with the additional work. In a calm tone, you would say:**

**Level 1:** Start with a Positive Comment.

> *"Your store was recommended to me based on the quality of service and the excellent reputation it has"*

**Level 2:** Give a clear explanation of the problem/issue

*"I was given an original quote that I agreed to, but at the end of the repairs, I was given a different figure for additional repairs that I did not approve of and that I should have been allowed to consider before the repairs went ahead".*

**Level 3:** Explain how the problem is affecting you emotionally/ physically.

*"I am very upset and do not believe that I have not been treated according to the policies outlined by Consumer Affairs." "I also feel that I have been taken advantage of".*

**Level 4:** Consequence or loss to the person if the problem continues.

*"If I were to make a formal complaint to Consumer Affairs, I am sure that they would agree that I should have been informed of the additional costs and that this was my decision to make. As a result, I will only pay for the amount on the original quote."*

If the Store Manager persists on you having to pay for

the latest quote, you would say:

> *"If you do not accept payment for the original quote, then you will leave me with no choice but to make a formal complaint to Consumer Affairs and write a poor review about the negative experiences I have had dealing with your organisation".*

**9. You invite your friends to your dinner party, but they don't show up or call you to cancel or apologise. In a calm tone:**

**Level 1:** Start with a Positive Comment.

> *"I have a lot of respect for you and our friendship and feel I need to bring this up with you".*

**Level 2:** Give a clear explanation of the problem/issue.

> *"I was really looking forward to you coming to my dinner party, and so were many of our mutual friends, and you didn't even show up."*

**Level 3:** Explain how the problem is affecting you emotionally/ physically.

*"The fact that you didn't even call me to inform me that you were not coming and didn't apologise upset me a lot, as that is something that I would never have done to you out of respect for your feelings."*

**Level 4:** Consequence or loss to the person if the problem continues.

If your friend becomes defensive and refuses to take responsibility for her actions, then you could say this:

*"The fact that you will not take responsibility for your behaviour shows your little respect for me. If we cannot have a relationship based on respect, then I don't think we can continue to be friends".*

**10. You are participating in a work meeting with all your work colleagues and manager present. One of your colleagues asks you a question you do not know how to answer. In a calm tone, you would say:**

**Level 1**: Start with a Positive Comment.

*"That is a great question"*

**Level 2:** Give a clear explanation of the problem/issue.

*"I have only been researching this topic briefly, and there is much to cover. The purpose of this meeting is to give you a general overview of the topic only, but I appreciate your interest in learning more, and I will definitely, get back to you with an answer".*

**Level 3:** Explain how the problem is affecting you emotionally/physically.
(This level is not necessary for this scenario)

**Level 4:** Consequence or loss to the person if the problem continues.

You would only need to communicate at this level if the colleague who asked the question complained about you not knowing the answer. In this case, you would reply in a firmer tone with:

*"As I mentioned, I have not had an opportunity to cover more than I am sharing in this meeting, and I will answer your question after I have done more research on the topic".*

## ✏️ Activity 5.0 – Basic Formula
### Scenario A
Apply the basic formula to the following scenarios.

Apply the formula to the following scenarios. Come up with your own responses based on the formula i.e. *1. Positive Comment, 2. Problem, 3. How the problem is affecting you, 4. Consequences, 5. Negotiation (if needed).*

1. Mark is returning a DVD to a shop—Amy is the shop assistant. It was a surprise present for his partner. When they tried to play it, it kept freezing. He has his receipt. Amy refuses to give me a refund and tells him she can only give him a credit to use in the store. What assertive approach should Mark take?

2. Dan is Nina's line manager. He is carrying out an annual appraisal, checking to see how things are going for Nina. Nina is very shy and friendly but gives short one-word or short-phrase replies. Nina is bored with her job and feels she'd like more responsibilities in her role. Dan knows that Nina is excellent at her job, and this is an opportunity for her

to say exactly how she'd like to develop her career. But Nina is reluctant to express what she wants. She's opened up in the past in other jobs and been disappointed and was also told off when she questioned things. What assertive approach should Neil take to help Nina feel comfortable enough to open up to him more?


3. Ian and Megan are co-workers designing a web page in their IT department. They are discussing various colour schemes and animations for a client. There is a brief sheet, but it is open to their creative flair. Ian keeps interrupting Megan, not really listening to her ideas. He isn't nasty he is just overenthusiastic and not very skilled at working with another person. Megan finds it hard to be heard and gets frustrated. What assertive approach should Megan take?


4. Neil is cold. His central heating is broken. He lives alone. Neil is calling to get his central heating fixed – he is on a plan he pays for once a year. He wants them to visit at a time that suits his diary, as he works daily. He is very good at asserting that he is cold and wants his heating fixed but is not good at asserting that it must be at a time to suit him. The discussion

seems to result in the appointment getting further and further in the future. Neil has never called before for a problem and pays a lot for the service. What assertive approach should Neil take?

5. Rebecca has approached Mark, who is not her line manager but above her. She wants to discuss with Mark how she felt when he undermined her during the team meeting that they were all a part of. She is particularly upset about the several sexist comments that he made. None of them were about her. When she gives Mark the feedback, he initially tries to play it all down. What assertive approach should Rebecca take?

6. Steve and Hilary are partners. Steve is upset about the state of their flat. He's been doing his best to tidy the flat for the last two weeks. They both have heavy workloads at work. Steve is starting to build resentment towards Hilary and has been sarcastically approaching the issue, which has only caused Hilary to become defensive and argumentative. He wants to approach Hilary in an assertive way to resolve the issue. What assertive approach should Steve take?

# 6.

## *Being Assertive in Your Relationships*

Assertiveness skills and communication skills come hand in hand. You need clear and concise communication skills to ensure that your message is understood, and you need assertiveness skills to ensure that the other person accepts the message. So, basically, you want to make sure that no barriers can stand in the way of achieving your goal. If you clearly explain what you need from the person (using communication skills), and tactfully deliver the message (using assertiveness skills), then there should be no reason why your message cannot be accepted other than the simple fact that the person does not want to accept it.

Assertiveness skills and effective communication are two important skills essential for a healthy personal relationship. Both parties need to communicate assertively and clearly to work through and resolve common relationship issues. Otherwise, problems are left hanging and unresolved. Long-term, unresolved problems can develop into resentment and unhealthy beliefs, eventually destroying the relationship. When you have healthy and open communication with your partner, your relationship will thrive and survive long-term. Ideally, both parties should have strong communication and assertiveness skills, but this is not always the case. It's more common for neither party to have strong assertiveness and communication skills. Often, this is because neither have learned how to be assertive, so neither can improve the communication between them for their relationship to improve. This is where your new assertiveness skills will come in handy.

To communicate effectively in a relationship, at least one person needs to be assertive, while the other should be open to learning how to be assertive. Communicating assertively with your partner can help them develop their assertiveness. However, if both partners lack assertiveness skills, it can be challenging. Sharing your assertiveness skills with your partner can improve communication between you both. If your partner already has assertiveness skills, learning these skills yourself can elevate your communication and relationship to a new level.

If your partner is unwilling to learn assertiveness skills, communication will be difficult, stressful, and ineffective. This can often result in futile arguments that lead to resentment and disconnection. How important is the relationship to them to make the necessary effort to learn assertive communication?

## Communicating Assertively with Family and Friends.

As mentioned earlier, not everyone will appreciate your new skills. Some people will embrace them, and others will dislike them. The people in your life who do not like your new assertiveness skills will likely be those who did not respect you in the first place. Unfortunately, you will only have two options with people like that: you can continue to assert yourself with them and hope that they will eventually come around to accepting your new skills, or you can gradually distance yourself from them. These people thrive on controlling, manipulating, and putting you down for their benefit.

Unfortunately, avoiding certain family members is impossible, even if you don't want them in your life. These individuals are typically disrespectful and mistreat you, expecting you to tolerate their behaviour. Keep your distance and, most importantly, don't give them too much information to use against you. Remember, only those you have a genuine relationship with deserve to have details about you and your life. Keep communication brief and general. Be prepared to assert yourself, as this will prevent them from continuously targeting you. Keeping a safe distance and confronting them assertively will protect you. After a few attempts at breaking down your "invisible" wall, they will eventually get the message, give up, and look for another victim. People like that usually do not change, and all you can do is exercise your assertiveness skills with them to protect yourself from them.

Here is an example of how you would assert yourself with someone who fits that description:

Consider this scenario an example: A family member you do not trust asks you about your work. The truth is that you have been facing some challenges at work and are considering leaving the job.

You may want to consider responding like this:

**Family member:** *"How's work been going?"*

**You:** *"Work is fine, but there are a few issues I am working on addressing".*

**Family member:** *"What kind of issues?*

**You:** *"Just minor issues (minimise the issue), what about you? How's work going? (divert the attention from you to them).*

To minimise the issue and shift the focus back to the other person, politely suggest that they mind their business. This also communicates that you don't trust them enough to share more details, especially since they have previously used information against you.

Remember, you should only share detailed information about your life with people you have tested and trust. These are individuals who have never used the information you shared against you. If someone doesn't meet these criteria, they should remain in the "acquaintance" zone. You should still be courteous and respectful, but they will only know the most basic information about you. While you may be unable to change certain family members to have a healthy and genuine relationship with you, you can protect yourself from negative behaviour by being assertive with them.

The typical things you will need to assert yourself against are;

1. Being falsely accused or blamed for something you did not do.
2. Being pushed to do something you do not want.
3. Being put down.

## 1. Being falsely accused:

If you are falsely accused of something you didn't do, simply correct the accuser with the facts. The only way to convince them of their error is to state the facts they are ignoring. No one can dispute the evidence. In this situation, you might want to say something like this:

**You:** *"That is incorrect. This is what actually happened. [Give them evidence to support your case]"*.

If the family member persists, don't argue, smile and say,

*"You can believe what you want, but that is the truth." Then you drop the argument.*

If the family member continues to argue, put your hand up and say,

*"There is no point in arguing; you can believe what you want, and I will believe what I want".*

(Walk away from the situation if the family member does not drop the argument and it escalates).

Remember, you cannot reason with someone with no intention of being reasonable. Engaging in an argument with such a person will only be futile, and you will gain nothing from it. By not engaging, you will disempower them, and they will be less likely to target you and undermine your self-confidence. Just because you cannot change a person doesn't mean you cannot stop them from targeting you and trying to destroy your self-confidence.

## 2. Being pushed to do something that you do not want to do:

When you haven't been assertive with family members and in your personal relationships, people expect you to always agree with them, accommodate their needs, and let them have their way every time. They may even push their demands on you, even when you try to assert yourself. It's important to recognise that this results from their bad habits, which may take some time to change. You need to persist and stand your ground. Eventually, the people who care about you will accept the new, assertive you.

## Broken Record Method

The 'Broken Record' method is a very effective tool to use with very pushy/persisting people. When you are using the Broken Record, you are conveying the same message in a different way each time until it's accepted. So, each time that the person tries to force their opinion or their way onto you, you would stand your ground and use different words and/or a different sentence structure to deliver your message.

Here is an example of how to apply the Broken Record technique.

If you feel pressured to do something you're not comfortable with, consider saying the following:

*"I'm not keen to do that",* or *"That isn't something that I would enjoy", "That's just not*

*something for me"*, or *"I'm not comfortable doing this"*, or *"I know I won't like that"* or *"I can see how you would enjoy doing that, but it's not for me"*. They are more likely to accept your response when you are firm and direct and don't beat around the bush.

If someone continues to insist on something, keep repeating the same message, perhaps in a different way. They might not like your response, but they will eventually accept it. For example, if someone keeps telling you to apply for a job you are not interested in.

**You:** *"I appreciate your help, but I don't think I would enjoy working in that line of work"*

**Family Member:** *"But you would be great in that role"*.

**You:** *"Thank you, but I know it's not something I'd enjoy doing"* (Broken Record)

**Family Member:** *"I think you should just try it before you make up your mind"*.

**You:** *"No, I know it's not for me."* (Broken Record)

When you keep the "gate" closed, others will persist. The more they realise that pushing does not work, the sooner they will accept "no" from you and stop pushing their point. But don't expect them to learn from the first time you stand your ground. Expect them to try several times. After all, some people are more persistent than others and will take longer to realise that when you say "no," you mean "no."

## 3. Being put down.

Another reason why it's important to assert yourself in your personal relationships is to address putdowns. Putdowns can be direct, such as "You're stupid," or indirect and subtle, like "You might want to pick an easier course to study." Whether the putdown is obvious or subtle, if you want the person to stop putting you down, you must deal with it assertively. It can be hard to tell if something is meant as a putdown, but you'll know it when it hurts. Speaking up is your signal if something doesn't sit right with you. Whether it was a misunderstanding or intentional, your assertive response will help you figure it out. Keeping quiet and internalising your hurt will only encourage the person to continue putting you down in the future.

When faced with a putdown, it's best not to respond with another putdown, as that would be aggressive. Instead, try responding more constructively.

When someone says something that upsets you, handling the situation calmly and respectfully is important. You can do this by:

1. Asking them specific questions to better understand what they meant by their statement,

2. Using evidence to correct their statement, and

3. Informing them of how their statement was hurtful and how much it upset you.

When someone criticises you, you might want to respond with something like:

*"What do you mean by that comment [putdown]?"* If the family member did not intend it as a putdown, you should ask for an apology and an explanation to clear the misunderstanding. If, on the other hand, the person meant to put you down, then you should expect something like this:

Family Member: *"I was only joking; you're too sensitive."* The person will try to dismiss it and blame you for being too sensitive. Often when people are caught, they typically try to backtrack. In this case, you would respond as follows:

*"I want to address something that has been bothering me. When you made that comment, it hurt my feelings. I disagree with what you said because [provide evidence]. Please be mindful of how you say things in the future so you don't hurt my feelings. How would you feel if I had said the same to you? Even if you meant it as a joke, please think before speaking in the future, especially since this has happened multiple times. I believe that a genuine apology and effort to stop putting me down will show the authenticity of our relationship, regardless of your intentions. I hope we can work through this and improve our communication."*

People who put others down usually do so to boost their ego or envy something about the other person.

If someone intends to hurt your feelings, for example, by not using the phrase "it's a joke" and expects you to respond passively, they will be surprised when you respond assertively instead. Here's how you could respond assertively:

Using the 5 Step Assertive Formula;

> **You:** (Level 1: Positive Comment) *"I want to have a healthy relationship with you, but..."*
> (Level 2: Explain the Issue) *"...you constantly put me down and ...."*
> (Level 3: Explain how the problem affects you) *"... Every time it hurts my feelings"*
> (Level 4: Consequence for continuing the action) *"If you continue to put me down and hurt my feelings, I will become resentful, and it will affect our relationship".*
> (Note: for this situation you would not need to apply Level 5 – Negotiate a solution for a win-win outcome, as change needs to happen from the other person, not from you, given that they're the one giving the putdowns.

If you find yourself constantly dealing with the same problem with a family member, to protect your well-being, you may need to consider changing the nature of your relationship with them to more of an acquaintance level. If that's not an option, you might have to end the relationship when you can no longer tolerate it.

## Being Assertive with Your Child

One of the most important skills required for effective parenting is assertiveness. Many parents struggle to assert themselves with their children because they are overly-pleasing and lack assertiveness skills.

### Parents who Over-pleasing

It can be challenging to avoid over-pleasing your child, especially when you're doing it to "keep the peace and avoid a conflict" or to compensate for not spending enough time with them or not giving them the attention they need. We might also over-please to protect our children's feelings, such as when they feel sad, upset, angry, hurt, or bored.

We all want our children to have positive experiences and avoid negative ones. However, by constantly trying to please them, we may prevent them from learning how to manage their negative emotions and develop the necessary skills to cope with challenging situations they will likely encounter as adults. One important skill in this regard is assertion.

It's important for children to learn to respect and understand healthy boundaries. Children who always get their way may have difficulty coping with not getting what they want as adults. On the other hand, children who are taught to respect boundaries are more likely to establish and expect healthy boundaries as adults. This, in turn, helps them develop healthy relationships, self-confidence, and happiness.

**Parents who Lack Assertiveness Skills**

How we communicate with our children is greatly influenced by the communication style we were taught by our parents and the parenting style we experienced in our childhood. People with aggressive or passive parents are likelier to adopt a similar communication style. Conversely, those with assertive parents are likelier to adopt an assertive communication style.

Remember: How you communicate with your children will influence their communication as adults and parents. Developing assertiveness skills when parenting is important, as your children learn from you. By being assertive, you can pass these skills on to them.

**Discipline and Assertion**

Discipline and assertiveness go hand in hand. Without assertiveness skills, disciplining your children will be extremely challenging, regardless of their age. The more you give in to them, the more demanding they will become. On the other hand, being overly aggressive may backfire, as they are likely to respond aggressively towards you as they grow older.

When you are assertive with your child, you teach them to respect boundaries, and other people's feelings, negotiate, problem-solve, and expect to be respected by others. A child is curious and constantly learning, and when you are assertive with them, they will also learn to be assertive. As you do not respond well to being communicated incorrectly, neither will your child. How would you respond if your boss barked instructions at you or yelled at you for not listening to them? Assertiveness is communicating respectfully while being mindful of not hurting the other person's feelings. This is why when your boss asks you to do something, they will do it correctly, not to upset or disrespect you. They have the right to tell you what is needed to address the problem, but you also have the right to be spoken to respectfully. So does your child. When you assertively speak to them, you will likely be met with a positive and less defensive response. Assertiveness reduces the risk of conflict, defensiveness, and the tug-of-war for power that can come with disciplining a child or teenager.

How you communicate with your child and the language you use to address a situation are crucial for achieving a positive outcome. If your body language and style of communication are aggressive or passive, you will instantly lose their respect and willingness to work with you. Aggressively approaching them increases the risk of being met with aggression and defensive behaviour. On the other hand, passively approaching them increases the risk of being ridiculed and disrespected. What you say and how you say it must be assertive.

Learning to assert yourself with your child can help build a strong, trusting relationship, reducing the likelihood of resentment often arising from conflicts.

## How to be Assertive with your Child

Parenting is one of the most important and challenging roles in life. A parent's main responsibility is to ensure their child develops the necessary skills to become decent, responsible, well-adjusted, confident, and independent. It involves more than just "babysitting," which, unfortunately, many parents tend to confuse with the role of parenting. Effective parenting requires effective discipline, and effective discipline requires assertiveness skills.

Children will respond well to discipline if it is delivered assertively. So, how do you deal with your child assertively? By: Communicating the request clearly and concisely.

1. Explaining the reasoning behind the request.
2. Provide a warning if they refuse to comply with your request.
3. Providing them with a consequence for not doing what you requested.

## Communicating the Request in a Clear and Concise Way

It is crucial to clearly and concisely communicate your request to avoid any misunderstandings. Children learn to manipulate (and become very good at it) early. That's why explaining what you want them to do or not to do as simply, briefly, and clearly as possible is important. You don't want them to use the commonly used excuses such as: *"I didn't understand what you wanted me to do", "You didn't tell me to do that," or "I didn't hear you say that"* or *"I didn't know you wanted me to do that".*

When giving a child an instruction, you need to:

Make sure you have their full attention. Some children may say they are listening but easily get distracted and only get half of your instructions.

Some children are visual learners and process information visually. For visual learners, it might be a good idea to ask them to visualise each step of the instruction to help them retain the information longer. Ask them to repeat your instructions. This will confirm that they fully understood your instructions and do not use it as an excuse.

**Provide them with the Reason for the Request**

As previously mentioned, providing a logical reason for doing or not doing something increases the likelihood of achieving the desired outcome. When you explain the importance of a task or action to a child, they are more likely to comply with your request. If someone asks you to do something without explaining why it's important and the completion timeframe, you probably won't prioritise it on your to-do list. The same goes for children of any age. When you explain the importance of completing a task within a certain time frame, you have a better chance of them following your instructions. You need to get them on board before you can get them to work with you.

**Provide them with a Warning if they Refuse to do what you request.**

It's always a good idea to explain to your child the consequences they will face if they don't follow your instructions. Give them a warning along with the instructions. For example, you can say, "If you don't do your chores after school, then you won't be allowed to use your device tonight." Once you confirm that they understand the consequences and what is expected of them, there shouldn't be any reason for them not to do what is asked. A mistake many parents make is giving their children too many warnings. Doing this will only result in the child constantly pushing the boundaries, not necessarily because they believe they will 'force' you to 'give in', but because they will enjoy the feeling of having that little power over you (even if they know it won't last long). They will not take your warnings seriously if you do not follow through with them. Children know how many warnings they can ignore before the situation becomes serious. How often have you found yourself saying, "I'm going to count to five, and if you don't do as I say, there will be a consequence," only to have your child quickly comply just before reaching five? Giving them only one warning before taking the next step is less stressful and more effective.

One important thing to remember about warnings is that you should only warn someone about something if they have not already been warned about it. For example, if you have already warned them about not doing the dishes, the next time they don't, you should not warn them again but instead go straight to implementing the consequence. "If someone understands the instructions and has already been warned, there is no excuse for not following the instructions. This leads us to the next point: people usually won't change unless they have a reason to, often to avoid a consequence.

## Provide them with a consequence for refusing to do what you have requested.

People are generally motivated by two main factors: passion and consequence. We tend to put effort and commitment into things we are passionate about, which makes us happy. We also put effort into things if we know we will face consequences if we don't. People are more likely to change their behaviour if they know they will have to face consequences for continuing that behaviour or if they will benefit from it. When changing your child or teenager's behaviour, you will have an easier time doing it when you give them a consequence for continuing that behaviour. So, if you remove a privilege from your child or teenager, you will have an easier time getting them to do what you need, such as chores, homework, and following the rules. Two important considerations when removing privileges are what to take away and for how long. When deciding which privilege to revoke, it's best to take away something they value, such as an activity or possession they enjoy. There is no point in taking away something they are not very interested in or do not value or need. It has to be something they will miss or be impacted by when they lose it, such as their favourite movie or program, skateboard or bike, or favourite device or activity.

## Consequences and the Highly Creative Child

Your child's personality will greatly affect how they respond to your discipline. A child who seeks rewards and positive attention will likely be much easier to discipline. They are the type of children who respond well to 'reward charts,' 'pocket money,' or when they have 'disappointed' you. This is because highly creative children are driven by recognition and achievements. Unfortunately, the child who is most likely to be the most challenging for you is the highly creative child. This is because they are typically children who don't need as much positive attention from others. They prefer their own company to that of other people. "They don't feel the need to please, so they are the type of children who are more likely to respond better to receiving a consequence for their actions than to a reward. This doesn't mean that they wouldn't appreciate praise or a reward, but when it comes to changing their behaviour, they will respond better to a consequence than to a reward unless it is something that they are passionate about having. Highly creative children need instant gratification; they find it difficult to wait for their reward. So, if you want to change their behaviour by using a reward, you will need first to figure out a reward they really want and, second, a reward they will not have to wait too long to receive. Remember that certain rewards may not be as effective next time if a child loses interest in them. Highly creative children often switch from one activity to another, constantly seeking stimulation. One minute, they may be deeply engaged in something, and the next minute, they may have moved on. Highly creative children often become bored quickly with things they have learned and worked out. They are more interested in learning how to use something than playing with it, so they easily discard toys. But as I mentioned earlier, they will respond well to losing something important to them at that time. For example, if they are playing a video game when you want them to do or not do something, taking away the video game immediately after they have not responded to your warning is the action you need to take.

Don't take away the electronic device they were using hours or days ago because it will not have as much of an effect motivating them. They are using that device because it is making them happy right now. They won't care about losing that device when they are no longer interested. So, unlike other children, who usually have a higher attention span and can become attached to something for a longer period, highly creative children are only going to respond to something they care about 'right now'. You will find that this theory also applies to teenagers. Here are some examples of what you can use as consequences to discipline your child:

- Their favourite toy.
- A program or movie they love to watch.
- A game they love to play.
- Missing out on their favourite dessert.
- Missing out on a trip to the park/ skate park.
- Their skateboard or bike.
- Next-door neighbour/ friend coming over to play.
- Their pocket money.
- Attending/having a playdate.

Here are some examples of what you can use as a consequence to discipline your teenagers:

- Pocket money
- Time on the internet.
- Their phone/ IPAD
- Restrictions on their computer
- Ride to their friend's place/school (if they usually catch the bus).
- Friend staying over.
- Favour for them.

## Concern about hurting your child/ teenager's feelings.

It can be challenging to take away privileges or let your child face the consequences of their actions, especially if they are not accustomed to being disciplined in this manner. One of the major obstacles for parents when it comes to disciplining their children is being overly concerned about their feelings. "The Over-Pleasing Parent"

The second biggest challenge is handling the manipulation and tantrums that can arise when privileges are taken away from children accustomed to getting their way for a long time. As mentioned earlier, it's important for children to learn that in the real world, they won't always get what they want, they'll need to be patient, and they'll have to do things they may not want. This is the reality of adult life. Teaching them this through effective disciplining will prepare them to deal with negative situations that will inevitably bring negative emotions. For example, having to do a task at work that they don't enjoy, missing out on a concert because they did not have enough money, or losing a friendship because they did not put in the effort. These experiences are necessary to develop the skills needed to cope with everyday life stressors and build problem-solving skills for adulthood. If you're hesitant to discipline your child because you're worried about hurting their feelings, it's important to remember that if you're doing it in the right way, the only thing upsetting them is not getting their way, not the way you're disciplining them. It's important to realise that effective discipline will also teach them about the realities of adult life.

## Dealing with the tantrums and aggression.

When you first start setting boundaries, you should

anticipate facing tantrums and manipulation. Your child or teenager is accustomed to getting their way, so they may expect you to give in because it has always worked for them. Unfortunately, you will have to endure some resistance before you can establish peace. Perseverance and consistency will eventually lead to a more peaceful and calm environment. This process may take a few days to a couple of weeks, depending on the child's character, age, and how long they have been allowed to have their way. However, once they realise that you are sticking to your rules and that their attempts to manipulate or throw tantrums are no longer effective, they should eventually accept your new disciplinary approach. If you are a passive person, this is the stage that you will find most difficult, especially if your child/teenager tends to become aggressive. Here is a tip on how to deal with this should it happen:

*TIP: When your child or teenager has a tantrum or becomes aggressive, tell them that the more aggressive they become or continue their tantrum, the more time you add to their consequence.*

For example, if a young child is having a tantrum or being aggressive, you should say:

> *"I will take it away [privilege] regardless of your tantrum/aggressive behaviour, and the longer you keep this tantrum/aggressive behaviour up, the longer you will lose it [privilege]. So, instead of losing it for 15 minutes, you will lose it for an extra 15 minutes if you continue to carry on like this. It's your choice; lose it [privilege] for 15 minutes only or double or triple the time."*

For instance, if a teenager starts to act aggressively, you should speak to them in a firm tone of voice:

"You did not do what I asked you to do (behaviour you are correcting), and I warned you that you will lose internet time (privilege). Your aggressive behaviour will not change anything; the more you continue that aggression, the longer you lose the internet (privilege). It's your choice." You may need to do this repeatedly to break their habit of using aggression to force you to give in to them. Some habits are tougher to break than others, but with your persistence, they will eventually break.

## Dealing with the manipulation.

Many children and teenagers try to avoid getting into

trouble by manipulating the situation if it has worked for them. We have previously discussed some common forms of manipulation they may use, such as pretending they weren't aware of the problem or claiming they didn't hear or understand you. When this happens, it's important to stand your ground and remind yourself that they did understand your instruction and the consequences at the time. Don't be fooled by their manipulation. Trust your memory of what you said and did at the time. It's easy to doubt yourself when confronted, but staying firm is crucial. It's important to ensure the recipient understands what you're saying when giving instructions. Accusing them of manipulation will only escalate the situation and give them an opportunity to avoid facing the consequences.

Just concentrate on staying on track and the behaviour that needs correction. For example, you might want to say something like this:

*"You didn't do your chores, and I warned you that you would lose computer time. That's final. You can argue with me all you want, but it won't change my mind. I will follow through with that consequence, and the longer you argue, the longer you will lose time on your computer."*

## Following through with your warning.

If you fail to follow through with your warnings, your child or teenager will continue to push the boundaries and not take your actions seriously. Inconsistencies from you will only lead to more arguments, aggression, and tantrums, and you will not gain their respect in your parenting. If you are serious about improving their behaviour, they need to see that you are serious by following through with the consequences. Not following through with your warnings will empower them and make your life more stressful.

You need to:
1. Take away something they value and won't want to lose.

2. Don't argue with them; deliver your message assertively, using evidence to support your case if necessary.

3. Don't fall for their manipulation, and don't call them up on it.

4. Give them a warning, and follow through with the consequence if needed.

5. Don't match them on their aggression; instead, stay calm and stand your ground.

6. If their aggression or tantrums escalate, warn them that you will extend the duration of the consequence if they don't calm down. Follow through with that warning if necessary.

7. Point out where they went wrong, but do not criticise. Your issue is with their behaviour, not with them.

## ✎ Activity 6.0 – Basic Formula
## Scenario B

Write an assertive response to the scenarios below.

### SCENARIO 1:

Your mother wants you to come over to her house right away so you can help her sort through items she wants to sell at a garage sale. You have planned to spend the evening relaxing, taking a soothing bath, just lounging around because you've had a rough week at work.

### SCENARIO 2:

You planned to meet up with your girlfriend/ boyfriend to have a nice meal at a restaurant. You get there, but he/ she is late—*again*. Almost every time you have made plans in the past, he/ she has been 20 - 30 minutes late.

### SCENARIO 4:

Your teenage son/ daughter is known to get angry every time you try to tell him/ her to clean up his/ her room or to help her out around the house.

# 7.

## *Being Assertive in the Workplace*

If you were to ask yourself what aspect of your job is the most challenging, you would probably say that it is dealing with certain people, not the tasks, job responsibilities, deadlines, or the operational problems that come with the job. Dealing with certain people, such as customers, staff, supervisors, suppliers, management, or co-workers, is typically the most challenging part of a job. Many factors hinder the ability to get along with people and work with or for them. The following factors can contribute to interpersonal challenges: differences in personality, individual issues, varying approaches to handling situations and problems, diverse communication styles, and differences in capabilities. While you cannot change people, you can reduce the impact of their behaviour on you by being more assertive in your interactions with them. If given the opportunity, difficult people will attempt to manipulate, control, and disrespect you. However, when you respond to them assertively, they will soon stop targeting you and, unfortunately, find someone else to target instead. Being assertive takes away the power others were trying to use over you. As mentioned in previous chapters, their main motive for wanting to overpower and control others is to boost their ego. If you block someone from using their ego-boosting tactics by being assertive, they will stop trying to manipulate you because it's not working for them, and they do not like to feel powerless.

## How to be Assertive with Customers

Most customers are reasonable to deal with, but no matter what industry you work in, you can't avoid encountering unreasonable, aggressive, and difficult customers. These customers have likely been successful at getting their way with others, which is why they continue to use aggression, but there is a right and fair way of dealing with aggressive customers. The first important thing to understand when dealing with aggressive customers is the underlying reason for their aggression. Aggression is just a form of manipulation to intimidate you into giving the person what they want. The first step is to demonstrate that you are not intimidated by them, remain calm and stand your ground. Once they realise they have no power over you, their aggression should quickly de-escalate. When dealing with an aggressive or difficult customer, remember that they are likely just "all bark and no bite." Like you, this means they are bound by workplace customer service and civil societal rules. This means they are well aware of the consequences they would face if they crossed the boundaries set by our legal system. They might get away with yelling and carrying on, but they know that this is as far as they can go if they want to avoid a conviction or some other legal implication. It's important to remember that while it's not easy or enjoyable to endure verbal abuse, you do have the option to end the conversation with the customer if they are being verbally abusive and aggressive towards you.

Dealing with a customer complaint may be part of your job, but tolerating abuse is not. An employer who disagrees with this and fails to protect their employees from such behaviour is not someone you should work for. You have every right to be respected, protected, and supported in your workplace. So, remember your rights the next time you have to deal with a difficult or aggressive customer.

*How do you calm an aggressive customer?*

Sure, here is the revised text:

"Let them know in a firm and calm manner that you are more than happy to assist them, but they will need to calm down for that to happen. Avoid using negative words like aggression, anger, difficult, or unreasonable to describe their behaviour. Also, refrain from saying or doing anything that implies you are unwilling to help them with their problem. This is because you don't want to escalate the situation or want them to become defensive. Your goal is to calm them down and to achieve this; you must tell them that once they have calmed down, you can help them with their problem. This information is crucial because their aggressive behaviour intimidates you into giving them what they want. Merely telling them to calm down without expressing your willingness to help them resolve the issue will likely make them even more aggressive. If someone knows you are willing to help them, they shouldn't have any reason to continue their aggression. You don't want to aggravate them, so using the words 'calm down' rather than 'you are being aggressive' should give you a better chance of de-escalating their behaviour.

The second approach you need to take for them to remain calm is to tell them that you understand why they are upset and that you will do your best to help them. By showing them empathy, understanding, and a willingness to help, you stand a better chance of having them work with you rather than against you. A person who is in a calmer state is usually more reasonable and easier to work with. Although the outcome they want might not be possible, they are more likely to accept this when they are calm and more rational. This is why it is important first to get them to calm down before you try to tackle the problem with them. Once you have calmed the customer down and can engage in a rational discussion, you can start helping them with their issue. However, there may be situations where you cannot resolve their problem. How would you handle a scenario like this?

If you are unable to solve their issue, then to keep them calm, you need to approach it in this way:

*"I'm really sorry, but I do not have the power to make that decision. What I can do, however, is take the matter to my manager and ask them to*

> *look into it. I wish I could do more, but I'm the Customer Service Officer, not the Manager. I hope you can understand this."*

I clarified that I don't make the decisions and that my role is to pass their issue on to the manager. Communicating that a) I want to help them but don't have the authority to make decisions and b) I'm ready to escalate their concern to the right person should help keep them calm. Customers want their problems resolved, so if they know I'm trying my best to help them, they're less likely to take out their frustration on me.

*"What should you do if they don't calm down?"*

You can't reason with the unreasonable. If someone isn't calm and reasonable, let them know you will need to assist them at another time. Explain that the problem can't be resolved until it can be discussed in a rational and calm manner.

> *"I understand that you are upset, but I believe revisiting this discussion would be more productive when you feel calmer. I want to help, but I need you to be in a more composed state to do so."*

Customers usually want their issues resolved as soon as possible. Informing them that they need to wait unless they calm down will likely encourage them to calm down immediately. If they persist, you might need to use the broken record technique.

*What should you do if their aggression escalates after this?*

As a Customer Service Officer, you have limited options to control the situation. You can only deal with the problem to a certain extent before involving your manager in the matter. If necessary, your manager can make decisions and take further action, such as calling the Security Officer to assist. Your manager is responsible for keeping you safe. They should take control of the situation and handle it from there to ensure this. If a manager fails to do so and leaves the matter for you to deal with, especially when they know you don't have the authority to make necessary decisions or take required actions, they are not someone you want to work for.

As a manager, it is your responsibility to ensure the safety of your employees. You may need to take over for your Customer Service Officer. If a customer's behaviour escalates, you must warn them that you will call Security if they do not calm down.

*"If you calm down, I can help you with your problem. However, I must call security to escort you out if you cannot do so. As our Customer Service Officer has already informed you, we are willing to sit down and address your problem, but only if you calm down."*

Providing a consequence may be effective in helping de-escalate a customer's negative behaviour. If a warning does not work, it may indicate that the individual cannot control their behaviour for various reasons. In such cases, for the safety of other customers and staff, calling security to manage the situation may be necessary. There's only so much you can do to control a situation without putting yourself, the customer, other customers, and your staff at risk. It's not worth taking that risk, so rely on the available resources and don't feel like you have to handle the situation alone. You can only control what's within your power.

Aggression, as I mentioned at the beginning of this book, can be a deliberate form of manipulation or a symptom of anxiety and/or fear. When we fear the worst, our body goes into a 'fight or flight' state, preparing us to either run away or confront the threat. This response is driven by increased adrenaline, creating the urge to fight or flee. Unfortunately, some people struggle to control the urge to respond aggressively in certain situations. In these cases, it's best to reassure the person that you will do your best to resolve their problem, focus on calming them down, and avoid escalating the situation with aggression. Whether the aggression is a symptom or a form of manipulation, it's important to respond similarly. A customer who is aggressive due to 'panic' would usually start off calm and then become noticeably anxious when you stand your ground and assert yourself. This is because the panic is usually triggered by their fear of you becoming 'aggressive' towards them. Conversely, a customer who is aggressive in manipulation will likely start off aggressively and remain aggressive throughout the situation.

In summary, the steps you should take when dealing with a challenging customer are:

1. Calm them down by reassuring them that you are eager to assist in resolving their issue.

2. Further calm them down by showing empathy and understanding their frustration.

3. Take control of the situation by informing them that you cannot assist until they have calmed down.

4. Use the Broken Record technique if the person persists.
5. Call your manager if the situation gets out of hand.
6. If you are a manager and the situation gets out of control, then call Security.
7. If the customer can calm down, proceed to the problem-solving phase.

*What should you do if the customer calms down but you cannot assist them in resolving their problem?*

You may encounter circumstances where you cannot resolve a customer's issue due to specific company and industry regulations. As an employee, it is important to adhere to the policies and procedures that are part of your role. It is crucial to communicate to the customer that these rules are binding and no exceptions can be made.

You could inform them by saying something like this:

*"I'm really sorry, but these are the company rules, and I cannot break them."*

*[If the customer persists]: Use the Broken Record technique: "I'm sorry, I wish I could help you, but I don't make the rules."*

*[If the customer persists further]: Suggest that they forward their complaint to management: "All I can suggest is that you forward your complaint to my manager for them to review. Here are their contact details."*

## Asserting Yourself with Your Employer.

It's important to communicate effectively with your employer when asking for time off, a pay raise, changes in responsibilities, more or less work, extra resources, additional training, leave, entitlements, or a promotion. To improve your chances of success, it's important to approach these conversations assertively. Before doing so, it's essential to understand your rights in the workplace, including your employee entitlements and those outlined by Fair Work. Equipping yourself with this knowledge will increase your chances of achieving your goals and reduce the risk of being manipulated. One of the barriers that can prevent people from asking for what they want from their employer is the belief that they don't deserve it.

How can you ask for holiday leave you are entitled to when you don't think you deserve it? Or ask for a pay raise when you don't believe you are worth it? Regardless of your or your employer's opinions, you have the legal right to that entitlement. If you rarely receive criticism in your role, rarely make mistakes, meet your position's responsibilities, work at the required performance standard, and have received increased responsibilities, positive appraisals, and compliments, you have proven to be a valued and worthy employee. So, when requesting your entitlements, It is recommended to utilise the 5-Step Assertiveness Formula. For instance…

### Asking for a pay rise:

**You: (Positive comment)**
*"I enjoy my job and like working for this organisation."*
**(Issue/ problem)**
*"But, as you can appreciate, living expenses have increased, and I haven't had a pay increase in that time."*
**(Impact this is having on you)**
*"Trying to make ends meet is causing a lot of stress, not only for me but also for my family."*

**(Consequence to the employer if the situation does not change)**

*"As I have mentioned, I enjoy working here. However, if I cannot receive a pay raise, I have no option but to look for other employment for the reasons I have just explained to you."*


## Asking for a decrease in workload:

**You: (Positive comment)**
*"I like my role and working for this organisation"*
**(Issue/problem)**
*However, ever since Katie left the company, my workload has increased.*
**(Impact this is having on you)**
*"As a result, I've been feeling overwhelmed, and it's starting to impact my health."*
**(Consequence to the employer if the situation does not change)**
*"I don't think I can continue to handle this workload for much longer, and my doctor is worried about its impact on my health. I wanted to let you know that my doctor has suggested finding a less demanding job, and I'd like to address this before it becomes necessary. Is there a chance we could reduce the amount of work I'm doing?"*

## Asking for holiday leave:

**You: (Positive comment)**
*"We all work hard in the organisation, and although I don't want to put extra pressure on the team..."*
**(Issue/problem)**
*"It's been a while since I last took a vacation, and I really need a break."*
**(Impact this is having on you)**
*"I have been experiencing frequent headaches and have been struggling recently."*
**(Consequence to the employer if the situation does not change)**
*"I need to take some time off soon because I am concerned about my health."*


## Asking for more responsibility or to be considered for that promotion:

**You: (Positive comment)**
*"I have been serving as the Assistant Manager for five years and have thoroughly enjoyed my role."*
**(Issue/problem)**
*"I feel that I need more of a challenge and responsibility."*

**(Impact this is having on you)**
*"I have gained a lot of experience and knowledge over the past five years, but I feel that my role is no longer challenging or stimulating for me."*

**(Consequence to the employer if the situation does not change)**
*"I believe I am the best candidate for the Senior Management Role and would like to be considered. I enjoy working for this company and do not want to have to work for another company to feel fulfilled in my career."*

## Being Assertive in Meetings

You will find assertiveness skills very useful during a meeting when you are asked to do something you do not want to or do not have the time to do. When you have something to contribute to a meeting, someone interrupts or talks over you. Being assertive means standing up for yourself when you are being wrongly blamed for something you didn't do or didn't have the necessary information, resources, training, or experience to do it. Being assertive means asking to be treated with respect and fairness.

Below are some examples of how to approach the

following situations assertively:

## Being blamed for something that you did not do:

**You:**
**(Set the record straight)**
*"I don't know where you got your facts, but I am not to blame for that situation."*
**(Present your facts to prove your case):**
*"I was at a meeting at the head office then, so I was not involved."*
**(Set a boundary)**
*"While I understand the severity of the situation and have no problem admitting to my mistakes, I would appreciate it if you collected all the facts before accusing me."*

## Feeling pressured to do something that you don't want to do:

**You:**
**(Present your reasons for being unable to take on the task and support your case with facts)**
*"I am always happy to help the team and give my time, but I am currently working on Project A,*

*which takes up most of my time. So, at this stage, I am not in a position to take on more work."*

## When someone interrupts your conversation and doesn't allow you to contribute to the discussion:

**You:**
**(Assertive body language)**
Put your hand up to the person who has interrupted your conversation to stop them and say, *"Excuse me, I was talking, and you just interrupted me."*
**(Set a boundary)**
*"We all have something to contribute to the topic, and everyone should be allowed to share their opinions or concerns, including me. You have interrupted me previously, and I would appreciate it if, in the future, you allowed me to finish my conversation."*

## Feeling incompetent when asked to do something:

**You:**
**(Set the record straight)**

"I appreciate your faith in me taking over this project, but ..."

**(Present your facts to prove your case):** *"I've only been in the position for three months and haven't yet had the opportunity to gain the necessary experience."*

**(Set a boundary)**

*"If John is available to supervise my work, I will feel more confident to take on the task. Otherwise, I will have to decline the opportunity on this occasion."*

When you provide evidence to support your argument in most of these situations, you force them into a corner. Also, I didn't personally attack the person, even though they were aggressive towards me, nor did I respond aggressively. By setting boundaries, you are teaching the person to respect you, and in doing so, you are also teaching them to respect others. "If the person does not respond positively to your assertion, you may need to apply a consequence. For example, you could say, "If you can't see that you have been disrespectful, I might need to discuss this matter further with our supervisor."

## Being Assertive with Your Staff

Managing staff without assertiveness skills is extremely challenging. Employees require clear direction, guidance, supervision, performance management, and motivation from their manager to perform at the expected standard for their role. Different individuals may require varying levels of support based on their personality, learning capacity, experience, knowledge, confidence, work ethics, and attitudes. Remember, asserting yourself allows you to establish boundaries with your staff from the start. When you are confident and assertive, your staff are more likely to respect you and perform at their best. Otherwise, they may try to take control. Remember that you hold more power than you might realise as their manager.

*So, how can one become an assertive manager?*

Here are some instances where asserting yourself is necessary and how to do it, using the 5-Step Formula:

**A staff member is not performing at the expected standard. You have already discussed this issue with them.**

**You:**
**(Positive Comment)**
"You generally work well with other staff, are well-liked, and are always eager to take on any task given to you."

**(Problem/Concern)**
"I'm concerned that you're not consistently meeting deadlines."

(Affect it is having on company/you)
"When tasks are not completed within the required timeframe, it creates significant pressure on the team, and some of our clients have lodged complaints."

**(Consequence to Staff)**
"We have discussed this issue several times, and I believe we have resolved it. Unfortunately, the complaints persist. I think the organisation has done everything it can to assist you. If the problem persists, the organisation will have no choice but to place you on a performance management plan."

**A staff member is not following your instructions. This has occurred a few times; this is your first discussion with them.**

**You:**
**(Positive Comment)**

*"Overall, you perform at the expected standard in your role, and I have no complaints about your performance."*

**(Problem/ Concern)**

*"I am concerned that you are not always following my instructions when I give them to you."* [give a few examples to support your case]

**(Affect it is having on company/ you)**

*"I appreciate your initiative, but it's important to follow the instructions I give you. It's disrespectful when you don't follow my instructions. While I'm open to more efficient ways of doing tasks, as your manager, I make the final decision."*

**(Consequence to Staff)**

*"This has happened a few times, and since this is the first instance I am bringing it to your attention, I will only issue a verbal warning."* [If this were the second discussion, you would inform them about the next step, a performance management plan.].


**A part-time employee has been taking excessive time off, causing strain on the team.**

**You:**
**(Positive Comment)**

*"You've been with the organisation for three years and consistently performed at a high level."*
**(Problem/Concern)**
*"My only concern is that you have been taking much time off work lately."* [give a few examples to support your case]
**(Affect it is having on company/you)**
*"Unfortunately, we are already short-staffed, and it is starting to pressure the team."*
**(Consequence to Staff)**
*"If you struggle to handle your workload, please let me know so I can support you. I'm willing to assist you to the best of my ability, but I also have responsibilities to other staff and the organisation, so there may be limits to the help I can provide."*
[You are providing the person with an opportunity to accept your offer of assistance and rectify their behaviour]

**A staff member has filed a complaint against another staff member regarding their performance and lack of teamwork. This is the first time they have brought the issue to your attention.**

**You:**
**(Positive Comment)**

*"Thank you for bringing this issue to my attention."*

**(Problem/ Concern)**

*"To ensure fairness for both parties, I propose we schedule a meeting for the three of us. This will allow you and Karen to voice your concerns and collaborate on finding a solution. I recommend that both of you bring any evidence you have, as it will help resolve this matter."* [In this instance, there is no need for any consequences]

> ✏️ **Activity 7.0 – Basic Formula**
> **Scenario C**
> Apply your assertive response to address the scenarios below.

1. During a team meeting, Karen speaks at length, providing excessive detail beyond the relevant points. This behaviour detracts from the value of her comments. Karen is well-intentioned, but her communication style can be overwhelming for everyone else in the meeting. It's important to address the agenda items in this meeting, as there may not be another opportunity to discuss them for weeks. Should I address this behaviour during the meeting? If so, what should I say? Alternatively, would speaking to Karen privately after the meeting be more appropriate? If so, what approach should I take? If neither option seems suitable, what would be the best course of action and why?

2. As a team member, not the team leader, a colleague has failed to complete an important part of the project on time, impacting the deadlines for

the entire team. This situation requires me to stay back at work to meet my deadlines, and I am concerned that the quality of my work may suffer due to the short time frame. This is the third time this colleague has failed to complete a project on time. Should I address this with my colleague directly or speak to my manager? How should I convey my concern assertively?

3. How would you assertively respond in that situation When discussing something important with someone, and it seems like they're not listening? Would your response differ if the person is your boss, significant other, friend, or family member?

4. The meeting is lengthy and confusing, leaving you with questions and issues about the presentation while no one else has spoken a word.

5. After my idea was rejected in a meeting, one of the group members made personal and unjust remarks that really upset me. What assertive response should I give?

# 8.

## *How to Assert Yourself with Difficult People*

### The Perfectionist

A perfectionist is someone who refuses to accept any standard less than perfection. We have all encountered a perfectionist at some point in our lives, whether in our personal or professional lives. Perfectionists can be challenging to work for, work with, and live with. They often have good intentions but may use the wrong approach. While this chapter focuses on learning to assert yourself with difficult people like perfectionists, it does not delve into perfectionism. If you're interested in learning more

about perfectionism, there is a link to an interesting article at the end of this section.
https://www.healthcentral.com/article/20-signs-you-might-be-a-perfectionist

If you want to assert yourself with a Perfectionist, it's essential to understand their characteristics and behaviour to avoid taking their criticism personally. Here are some typical traits of a perfectionist.

1. **They have difficulty accepting being "second best" in any endeavour, even those they aren't really interested in.** They are highly competitive and can't stand to lose...at anything.

2. **Some individuals may avoid participating in activities or tasks if they know they won't be the best at them.** For instance, if someone excels at basketball but is only average at baseball, they might decline to play baseball, even in a casual setting, if they won't be the best on the team.

3. **They would rather give up on a task than not do it perfectly.** If they arrive late to a meeting, they won't go in. They won't bother handing it in if they don't think their report is perfect. They won't waste time trying if they can't do it perfectly."

4. **They sacrifice their own well-being to make something perfect.** They might skip eating or sleeping to continue working on a project because it isn't perfect yet.

5. **They believe there is a "right" and "wrong" way to do things instead of considering multiple approaches to achieve the same result.**

6. **They don't accept in-betweens.** Everything is either perfect or a failure. They don't believe that anything can be "okay." If they have not achieved perfection, they have failed. There are no grey areas in their life, only black and white.

7. **They are highly critical of mistakes.** They might be extremely detail-oriented because the final project must be correct, and every detail along the way must also be perfect. They notice any mistake or error, whether they made it or someone else did.

8. **They obsess about previous mistakes,** mulling over what they did and didn't do correctly. They worry that they did not do enough or did something wrong.

9. **They become defensive if anyone points out any errors** or criticises their work because it implies that they were not or are not perfect.

10. **They seek recognition.** They want everyone to think highly of them and be happy with what they have accomplished or done. They become stressed/ defensive if someone is not pleased with their work.

11. **They are judgmental and critical of others.** They want perfection in what they do and everything around them. They criticise any errors made by those around them.

12. **They have a difficult time emotionally connecting with other people.** Because they have an intense need to be accepted and a great fear of rejection, they might find it easier not to connect and, therefore, not risk rejection.

13. **They know achieving perfection is impossible and that their efforts are harmful to them.** Even so, they can't seem to stop themselves because the results would be disastrous. They can't imagine living with themselves if they don't try to be perfect, and they are sure that their world will fall apart if they stop trying.

14. **They take it very hard when they don't achieve perfection.** They struggle to deal with anything less because perfection is so important to them. When faced with challenges or mistakes they have made, they become dejected.

15. **They continue working on a project long past when it was complete, or others would have stopped.** That's because no matter how long they work, in their eyes, it is never quite done. There is always one more edit, change, and finishing touch. They will stop when it is "perfect."

16. **They feel relieved when someone else fails.** Although they know they shouldn't, seeing someone else make a mistake or fail at a task makes them feel better, at least for a little while. It reinforces that they are "the best."

17. **They find it very difficult when others see they make a mistake.** They might overreact by crying, yelling, screaming, making excuses for their mistakes, or blaming others.

18. **They think asking for help is a sign of weakness.** They believe that if they can't do it all, they can't be perfect, which isn't acceptable.

**19. They do only things that have a purpose.** They don't enjoy doing pointless hobbies. Instead, everything they do has a purpose in their life.

**20. They have a strong need to be in control.** When working on a group project, they naturally take the lead and assign tasks to everyone else. They often take on extra work to ensure everything is done correctly, as they believe in the motto, "If you want something done right, do it yourself." They struggle to work in a group if they are not in control. Living or working with a perfectionist can be extremely challenging and harm your self-esteem. Some of the behaviours of a perfectionist that you might find most difficult to deal with include Their high, unrealistic standards.

1. Their criticalness of others.
2. Their need to micromanage and to be in control.
3. And blaming others for their mistakes.

## Being Assertive with a Perfectionist

Two key steps to take when dealing with a perfectionist are: 1) Gather your own facts before conceding that you are at fault, and 2) Present your argument using these facts. Remember, just because someone is upset with you does not mean that they are right and that you are wrong. They might be upset based on their own assumptions, not facts. Presenting them with the facts should help you win your argument. Not standing up for yourself to avoid a conflict or prevent further upset will only encourage them to continue the same behaviour towards you, which may even worsen. This behaviour can be very stressful to tolerate in the long term, not to mention the damage it can cause to your self-confidence and mental health.

*Let's explore some examples of asserting yourself with a perfectionist by addressing the four common behaviours.*

### 1. Imposing their high, unrealistic standards.

**(Collect the facts):** First, ask yourself the following questions to determine if what they are asking you to do is a normal expectation and standard.

- Is there sufficient time to complete the task when they expect you to?

- Are most people with experience, skills, and knowledge similar to yours able to achieve the expected standard and/or timeframe expected of you?

- Is what is expected of you possible to complete with the resources you have available?

- Have you had sufficient training to complete the task?

It's important to gather evidence that supports your reasons for not meeting someone's expectations. This will help you determine if you are in the right or wrong, and it may also prompt the other person to consider facts before making assumptions in the future. Additionally, it could be beneficial to guide them in setting realistic standards and expectations.

As an example, you would say:

**You:** *"This project should normally take five days to complete, and it would have been done by that deadline had I not been pulled away from the project to resolve the issue in the Operations Department".*

**Person:** *"Yes, I know, but you should have still been able to complete it in five days".*

**You:** *"(Broken Record) As I have said, I did not have the time to complete it by that deadline."*

## 2. Criticising you.

**(Collect the facts):** Correct the person with facts.

Perfectionists tend to overlook the positives and instead focus on the negatives. As a result, they may criticise you for something minor that isn't worth mentioning or for something based on their opinion rather than facts. While it's important to consider constructive criticism, it's not healthy to accept unjustified criticism. If someone criticises you for something minor that has had no impact on them or anyone else, you can respond by pointing out the facts, for example:

**You:** *"Yes, we had a couple of hiccups, but overall, the meeting went very well, and we received great feedback (facts)"*

**Person:** *"Yes, but if we had not forgotten to do*

*Section 1.2, then we wouldn't have had these hiccups in the first place".*

**You:** *"This minor issue had no negative impact on the outcome [put it into perspective]".*

If the person criticises you for something that is not based on facts and solely on their own opinion. As an example, you might want to say something like this:

**You:** *"Can you please give me an example of how you came to that conclusion [facts]?"*

**Person:** *"It's just something I've noticed lately; I can't think of any examples right now".*

**You:** *"While I am always open to constructive criticism, I need facts to consider it; otherwise, it's just based on your own opinion, isn't it?"*

3. **Micro-managing and taking control.**

Perfectionists derive their sense of worth from their achievements, accomplishments, and productivity. When they are responsible for something, they feel that they are entirely accountable for achieving the desired result, and as a result, they will exert complete control to ensure that they do not fail. Failure is not an option for them, compelling them to seek control and micromanage. Working for perfectionists can be extremely stressful and unfulfilling, particularly when you are more likely to receive criticism than praise and be undermined.

*"How do you assert yourself with a perfectionist?"*

You may not be able to completely stop them from micro-managing your work, but you can certainly reduce the amount of micro-management. For this to happen, they will need to give you the opportunity to prove yourself and develop enough trust in you to let go. The next time someone attempts to micromanage your work, you may want to consider saying something like this:

*"I understand that your role is to ensure the project runs smoothly, but I've got it under control, and I know I can come to you if I have any problems that I can't handle. I have always met the deadlines on all my projects, [Facts], and I'm sure I will do the same with this one."* [Here,

*you remind them of your ability to build trust.].*

**Person:** *"Yes, I know that, but I still need to know where you are at with the project at all times."*

**You:** *[Broken Record] "It's okay, I have everything under control, and I will ask for your help if needed."*

You may need to use this script whenever someone tries to micromanage your work. You can also use the same script with someone who has perfectionistic tendencies in your personal life. Doing this lets them know you are in control of the situation or activity, and they are your backup if needed. Over time, gaining their trust should help you regain control over certain aspects of your life. Submitting to their controlling behaviour will only encourage them to take more control.

### 4. Blaming you for their mistakes.

Perfectionists strive to achieve 100% in everything they do. When they make a mistake, they tend to be hard on themselves. They often have a bad habit of blaming others for their mistakes to cope with this. For instance, they might say, "I took the wrong turn because you distracted me with your talking," or "I didn't do well on the test because you and your friends made too much noise and kept me up all night. "You might never convince a perfectionist to take accountability for their mistake, but you can end the argument without taking the blame. Let's use the example of the person taking the wrong turn.

**Person:** *"I took the wrong turn because you distracted me with your talking"*

**You:** *"You might have been distracted when you took the wrong turn, but you didn't tell me that my talking to you distracted you. [You are not directly blaming them but also informing them that you were not to blame either].*

As I've mentioned, reasoning with someone who refuses to be reasonable and accept logic is impossible. Even if you point out that they're not taking responsibility for their actions, they would deny it and become defensive because they can't admit to not being 'perfect' or handle 'imperfection'. Here is another example.

**Person:** *"I didn't do as well as I could have on*

***the test because you and your friends made too much noise and kept me up all night".***

Again, they are unlikely to admit they're wrong, but you don't have to accept the blame. "If we kept you up all night, you could have told us to keep it down or go downstairs to sleep in the spare bedroom. Don't forget that you have other options. Besides, you still got a high enough score on your test to pass the unit, even if you could have done better. Your need for 100% was not necessary or critical." When dealing with a perfectionist, it's important to remind them that they have options and that achieving less than perfection is still a success. it's important to understand that you can't change their behaviour because perfectionism is often an unhealthy coping mechanism they use to deal with their insecurities. Instead of taking their criticism or undermining comments personally, avoiding falling victim to their controlling tendencies is best. Many people make the mistake of trying to avoid criticism by giving in to their controlling behaviour. While you may not be able to avoid their criticism entirely, you can protect your self-esteem by only considering constructive criticism supported by facts.

## The Psychopath:

A psychopath is a person with a personality disorder characterised by persistent antisocial behaviour, impaired empathy, and bold, egotistical traits. ([Wikipedia](Wikipedia))

The twenty traits on the Hare Psychopathy checklist are:

1. Pathological lying
2. Glib and superficial charm
3. Grandiose sense of self
4. Need for stimulation
5. Cunning and manipulative
6. Lack of remorse or guilt
7. Shallow emotional response
8. Callousness and lack of empathy
9. Parasitic lifestyle
10. Poor behavioural controls
11. Sexual promiscuity
12. Early behaviour problems
13. Lack of realistic long-term goals
14. Impulsivity
15. Irresponsibility
16. Failure to accept responsibility
17. Many short-term marital relationships

18. Juvenile delinquency
19. Revocation of conditional release
20. Criminal versatility

The Hare Psychopathy Checklist-Revised (PCL-R) categorises these traits into four factors: **interpersonal, emotional, lifestyle, and antisocial.** If you would like to learn more, click this link: https://www.learning-mind.com/hare-psychopathy-checklist

**The Narcissist:**

The common traits of Narcissistic Personality Disorder (NPD) include grandiosity, lack of empathy, and a need for admiration. Individuals with this condition are often described as arrogant, self-centred, manipulative, and demanding. They may also have grandiose illusions and believe that they deserve special treatment. While "narcissist" is a word used a lot these days, the characteristics typically begin in early adulthood and must be consistently evident in multiple contexts, such as at work and in relationships. People with NPD often try to associate with individuals whom they perceive as being above the average person or gifted to enhance their own self-esteem. They constantly seek excessive admiration and attention from others and, as such, cannot tolerate or accept criticism or defeat. Symptoms may vary from person to person, but the most common symptoms include:

- Being overly arrogant, exaggerating their achievements
- A grandiose sense of self-importance
- A sense of entitlement to special treatment
- Exploitation of others.
- Envious of others
- Lack of empathy for others
- Looking down on others as inferior
- Monopolising conversations
- Impatient, angry, unhappy, depressed, or has mood swings when criticized
- Easily disappointed when expected importance is not given
- Always craves for "the best" in everything
- Has a very fragile self-esteem

If you would like to learn more about Narcissistic Personality Disorder, you can read the article 'All

About Narcissistic Personality Disorder' by Dr. Jeffrey Ditzell (Psych Central) click this link: https://psychcentral.com/disorders/narcissistic-personality-disorder

## Being Assertive with a Psychopath or a Narcissist

*How can you assert yourself when dealing with a psychopath or a narcissist?* The answer is - you don't.

Some people, such as narcissists or psychopaths, cannot be influenced through assertiveness. This is because they lack the capacity for empathy and taking responsibility for their actions. Psychopathy and Narcissism are both personality disorders, unlike certain personality traits, bad habits, and unhealthy coping mechanisms. Personality disorders cannot be changed. The best way to protect yourself from falling victim to a narcissist or psychopath is to look out for the signs and not to become involved with them in any shape or form.

## Being Assertive with an Emotionally Sensitive Person

It is easy to be assertive with another assertive person. However, being assertive with someone who is emotionally sensitive is challenging. The goal of assertiveness is to reach an agreement or find a solution. This can be difficult when the person you are assertive with cannot be open, honest, or cope with constructive criticism. For assertion to be effective, both parties need to be honest with each other and prepared to share and accept constructive criticism to achieve a win-win outcome.

*How can you assert yourself with an emotionally sensitive person who takes everything negatively?*

Remember to communicate the purpose of the discussion, how the other person will benefit from it, and that your intentions are good. Here are some examples:

If you need to address the unequal division of household chores with your emotionally sensitive roommate, you could say:

**You:** [5-Step Formula]

**(Positive Comment)**
*"I really enjoy living with you. You've been a great friend and support whenever I needed it. For this reason, I don't want you to take what I am about to say the wrong way. I know that this discussion will only strengthen our friendship."*

**(Issue/Problem)**
*"I understand that you work long hours and are also busy with your university course, and I know it's not your fault. However, I was hoping we could work together to solve the household chore situation. I've been busy too, but the chores still need to be done."*

**(Impact on you)**
*"I don't mind doing household chores, but lately, I've been feeling really tired and overwhelmed by it."*

**(Consequence to them)**
*"I value our friendship and don't want anything to come between us. I believe we can find a solution together."*

**(Negotiate Solution)**
*"Since you're so busy and don't have time to do your share of the chores, maybe you could consider hiring a cleaner to do your share until you can manage to do it yourself. What do you think?"*

If you must address a performance issue with an emotionally sensitive staff member, you should approach the situation with care and empathy.

**You:** [5-Step Formula]
**(Positive Comment)**
*"I want you to know I am really happy with your performance. I don't want you to take what I am about to say personally, as I intend to address a minor issue. Once it is resolved, it will benefit both of us."*

**(Issue/ Problem)**
*"You seem to have a good understanding of the new system, but I noticed that there are some areas that you are struggling with. Everyone learns at a different pace, and I am not concerned about how long it takes you to pick it up. My concern is that I don't want you to feel stressed and to continue to struggle unnecessarily."*

**(Impact on you)**
*"I have been a little concerned about you, as I want my staff to enjoy their job and feel that their workplace is safe and healthy."*

**(Consequence to them)**

*"I also don't want this problem to affect your confidence."*

**(Negotiate Solution)**
*"So, I was thinking we could have [e.g., Lisa/ staff member] assist you with some of your job responsibilities over the next two weeks. This will give you more time to learn the new system without worrying about completing all your duties. You can then focus solely on learning the new system. I don't think you've had enough time to learn the system thoroughly. What do you think?"*

When being assertive with an emotionally sensitive person, it's important to ensure that they understand your good intentions. Instead of blurting out the problem right away, take the time to communicate your intentions first. At the end of the discussion, highlight how they will benefit from the solution to show that you genuinely care about not hurting their feelings.

## Being Assertive with a Stubborn Person

Dealing with someone who won't take 'no' for an answer can be challenging. First, it's important to understand the motive behind their stubbornness. It's often a form of manipulation. People who refuse to budge are usually accustomed to persisting until they get their way. Their goal is to wear you down in the hope that you will give in to them. For instance, it could be the stubborn customer who demands a refund and won't leave until they get it, the teenager who insists on going to a party despite being told 'no', or the partner who insists on renovating the kitchen despite budget constraints.

How can you persuade others to accept what you know is the most logical course of action?

You can do this by standing your ground, not giving in to manipulation, and giving them a consequence for persisting with their behaviour. Playing "arm wrestle" is not a matter where the strongest person wins. It's about showing them that you are not intimidated and will stand behind what you believe is the right thing to do, whether by principle, rule, or cause. If standing your ground does not work to get them to accept "no" as your answer, then you will need to take the next step of giving them a consequence for continuing to persist. Here are some examples of being assertive with a stubborn person in a work and personal situation.

**Workplace Example:**

**Example 1:** A customer is requesting a refund for an

item without proof of purchase, refusing to leave without it. You have explained the company's policy, but they are not accepting it. In this situation, you might want to say something like this: You would say:

**You:** *"I understand you're upset about purchasing a faulty item. Unfortunately, I cannot issue a refund without the receipt as proof of purchase. It's important to note that I don't have the authority to override company policies."*

**Person:** *"I purchased the vacuum cleaner from this store last week, so I have proof from my bank statement. This should be sufficient for me to receive a refund."*

**You:** *[Broken Record] "I've already explained that we can only process refunds with a receipt. Without a receipt, I'm unable to process a refund. However, I can take down your details and forward them to our head office. They will likely advise the same policy."*

If the person persists:

**Person:** *"If I don't receive a refund immediately, I will file a formal complaint with Consumer Affairs."*

**You:** *[Broken Record] "If you believe filing a complaint with Consumer Affairs will benefit your situation, please feel free to do so. However, they will likely require a receipt for a refund. I apologise for being unable to assist you, but I will pass on your details to our Head Office."*

(If a person becomes aggressive, warn them about the consequences.).

You would say:

**You:** "If you continue to be aggressive, I will have no choice but to call the security guard." If that warning does not calm the person, call the security guard.

### Personal Example:

**Example 2:** You do not approve of your teenage son or daughter going to a friend's party because you have been informed by another parent that this friend tends to get up to no good and that their parties are unsupervised. Your son or daughter persists, and the more you say 'no', the more aggressive they become.

**You would say:**

**You:** *"I already told you you're not attending that party. I disapprove of the lack of supervision and your friend's reputation. My responsibility as your parent is to ensure that you are safe, including making sure that you do not get influenced by others who do not have a good reputation."*

**Teenager:** *"But he doesn't have a bad reputation. Who told you he did?"*

**You:** *"It doesn't matter who told me; I still disapprove."*

**Teenager:** *"That's being judgmental. [Aggression is escalating]. I don't care what you say, I'm going, and you can't stop me."*

**You:** *"I have already confiscated your phone for two days. If you go against my rule, keep pushing this matter, and continue your aggression, I will confiscate your phone for a month. So, I advise you to drop it now because I will not change my mind."*

If your son or daughter's aggression escalates, then you should say:

**You:** *"I warned you about your aggression, and now you have lost your phone for an extra day. Keep your behaviour up, and you will lose it for a month. This is your last warning."*

Your son or daughter should calm down. If they don't, you must follow through with your warning.

> ✏️ **Complete Activity 8.0**
> **Use the Basic Formula in situations you have encountered in the past**

Remember the following situations: a time at work or in your personal life when you did not respond assertively or a situation where you plan to assert yourself. How should you have responded using your new assertiveness skills?

**1.** a) What happened? (what did the person say or do?)

b) What assertive response should you have given at the time (past) or planning to do now (current)?


**2.** a) What happened? (what did the person say or do?)

b) What assertive response should you have given at the time (past) or planning to do now (current)?

**3.** a) What happened? (what did the person say or do?)

b) What assertive response should you have given at the time (past) or planning to do now (current)?

**4.** a) What happened? (what did the person say or do?)

b) What assertive response should you have given at the time (past) or planning to do now (current)?

**5.** a) What happened? (what did the person say or do?)

b) What assertive response should you have given at the time (past) or planning to do now (current)?

# Conclusion

Assertiveness is essential for maintaining healthy relationships, both personally and professionally. It is a barrier against toxic individuals who can negatively impact your well-being. Strong self-esteem is crucial for mental health, and having toxic people in your life can erode it. This includes those who put you down, manipulate and control you, abuse and use you, blame and unjustly criticise you, and make you feel unvalued and unappreciated. Assertiveness allows you to remove these toxic individuals from your life. However, it is often misunderstood and resisted by those it affects, as it closes the door to their harmful behaviour.

Understanding your personal and work rights is the first step before attempting to assert yourself in a situation. Clearly understanding where you stand in every situation will make it easier to address it assertively.

Learning to be assertive doesn't have to be difficult. It basically involves expressing how you feel and what you need in a way that cannot be misunderstood, misinterpreted, or offensive to the other person. You need to know where you stand by understanding your rights, presenting your facts, expressing how the situation impacts you, and explaining how it will impact the other person if it continues. "It's simple!"

Remember, you can't reason with the unreasonable. You can use assertiveness skills, but the only option is to walk away if someone isn't willing to accept the facts. It's easy to understand something presented logically and backed up with facts, but someone who doesn't want to accept it will refuse. For instance, if your boss refuses to give you the pay raise you deserve, finding another job is best. Remember: "Practice makes perfect." Start by using your new skills with people you feel comfortable with. This will help you build confidence to use them with more challenging individuals. When you see positive results, it will encourage you to apply your skills in any situation. If your assertion doesn't work on some people, it may not be because you're doing it incorrectly but because they're stubborn. Some people might expect you to back down under pressure, but if you stand your ground, they'll learn to accept the new assertive you. Unfortunately, some people will never accept your new skills and won't change for a healthy relationship. In those cases, it might be best to distance yourself from them, as they may only want you in their life for the wrong reasons.

www.ingramcontent.com/pod-product-compliance
Lightning Source LLC
Chambersburg PA
CBHW070552010526
44118CB00012B/1298